D1474870

Order, Freedom,
and the
Polity
Critical essays on
the Open Society

George W. Carey
editor

University Press of America
The Intercollegiate Studies Institute, Inc.

Copyright © 1986 by

The Intercollegiate Studies Institute, Inc.

University Press of America,® Inc.

4720 Boston Way
Lanham, MD 20706

3 Henrietta Street
London WC2E 8LU England

All rights reserved

Printed in the United States of America

Library of Congress Cataloging in Publication Data
Main entry under title:

Order, freedom, and the polity.

Essays given at a conference on the open society,
held at Georgetown University in 1982, sponsored by
the Georgetown University Government Department and
the Intercollegiate Studies Institute.
Bibliography: p.
1. Liberty—Congresses.   2. Democracy—Congresses.
I. Carey, George Wescott, 1933-   II. Georgetown
University.   Dept. of Government.   III. Intercollegiate
Studies Institute.   IV. Title: Open Society.
JC571.O77   1986   323.44   85-26438
ISBN 0-8191-5155-6 (alk. paper)
ISBN 0-8191-5156-4 (pbk. : alk. paper)

Co-published by arrangement with
The Intercollegiate Studies Institute, Inc.

All University Press of America books are produced on acid-free
paper which exceeds the minimum standards set by the National
Historical Publications and Records Commission.

JC
571
.O77
1986

Contents

WILLIAM T. BOYCE LIBRARY
FULLERTON COLLEGE
Fullerton, California 92634

Acknowledgements

The essays contained in this volume are the product of a joint undertaking sponsored by the Georgetown University Government Department and the Intercollegiate Studies Institute (ISI).

Thanks are due to E. Victor Milione and John F. Lulves, Jr., President and Executive Vice President, respectively, of ISI; Karl H. Cerny, who was Chairman of the Government Department at the time these papers were delivered at Georgetown University; and Father Donald Freeze, S.J., Provost of Georgetown University, for their generous support, both moral and material.

I am very grateful to Michael Jackson, now of the American Enterprise Institute, for his invaluable assistance in handling virtually all of the administrative work involved in the 1982 conference on the open society held at Georgetown University.

I will be forever indebted to Mary Ehart, Special Projects Director of ISI, for her diligence in preparing this volume for publication. Her good sense and persistence have made this a far better volume than it would otherwise be.

--GWC

The Open Society:
An Introduction

George W. Carey

The term "open society" comes readily to mind when we attempt to differentiate between the liberal democracies of the non-communist world and totalitarian regimes such as the Soviet Union. Moreover, the concept of the open society – at least to judge from the way it is used in ordinary discourse – presumably embodies within it that which liberal democracies hold dearest, namely, the values, ideals and ways of life worth fighting and dying for. Thus, the ideological battle between the West and East is frequently pictured in terms of the closed versus the open society.

These observations, as commonplace as they may seem, lead to another, not so obvious, which provides the rationale for these essays: that is, the concept of the open society has, curiously enough, been relatively immune to critical examination. This is not to say that certain fundamental tenets and elements of the open society have not been the subject of critical inquiry, particularly those advanced by Karl Popper. Such, for example, is the case with regard to freedom of speech and expression. But for the most part they have been treated apart from the context of the open society doctrine. And this is no small matter because these discrete elements take on a different hue when viewed in the broader con-

text of the theory of the open society, particularly in light of its
assumptions about man, the nature of society and its ends and,
among other things, the role of reason and tradition.

The essays which follow examine the open society theory from a
variety of perspectives. They all ask and explore questions that certainly should make sensible individuals wonder whether the open
society, as some contend, is the crowning achievement of Western
civilization. For instance, what does it mean to speak of an open
society? What are the philosophical roots of the doctrine? Does the
theory really have a status apart from that of simply identifying
certain practices and beliefs that prevail in liberal democracies? In
what ways and to what extent can a society be open and still be a
society? Are there human needs and wants that cannot be met
without contravening the underlying tenets of the open society
theory? What, in other words, are the limits of openness? What is
the status of "truth" in the open society theory? What epistemologi-
cal assumptions seem to underlie the quest for truth in the open
society? Are these assumptions compatible with the requirements
of a healthy society? Does our thinking about open and closed
societies tend to extremes, so that we exclude those positions that
see the need for societies somewhere in between, i.e., societies
open in some respects and closed in others? And, in this connection,
to what extent do the principles of the open society theory simply
preclude any cloture for whatever reason?

Certain of these essays point to concerns that go well beyond the
adequacy of the open society theory to answer the critics and foes
of liberal democracy. To a great extent, these concerns relate to
the widespread and uncritical acceptance of open society doctrines
which have served to undermine and weaken the social fabric of
Western societies. As such, the open society theory represents an
insidious force within the walls, far more dangerous in many
respects than the enemy without.

This is enough to indicate that these essays are not what might
be called "standard fare." They do not, as is so frequently the case,
simply extol the virtues of the open society by way of contrasting it
with the closed society. Rather, each one points to serious concerns
or shortcomings in the foundations and principles of the open society doctrine. In so doing, they present us with an implicit warning:
liberal democracies need firmer moral and intellectual foundations
than the open society theory is capable of providing.

Order, Freedom,
and the
Polity

Critical essays on
the Open Society

Popper's Open Society: Limitations on Critical Reason

George Carey

The concept of the "open society" deserves close scrutiny from a variety of perspectives, particularly that conception advanced by Karl Popper in his monumental work, *The Open Society and Its Enemies*.[1] In saying this I am not unmindful that the term "Open Society" was first coined by Henri Bergson in his *Two Sources of Morality and Religion*.[2] However, Bergson's conception is essentially different from and, at points, even antagonistic to Popper's.[3] What is more, it falls into what can be termed a "take it or leave it" category: those who empathize with his approach and outlook find it heuristic and suggestive; those who do not can summarily reject it. But, by any standard, this is far from the case with Popper's conception, which has in recent decades become something of a model against which the "openness" of a society or regime is measured. Consequently, when we encounter the term "open society" in ordinary discourse, it is normally employed in the Popperian sense. Such is the case, to take but one common example, when our political leaders and editorialists contrast the "open society" of the United States with the "closed society" of the Soviet Union.

Now, Popper intended for the term "open society" to be used in

the manner it is today; that is, to distinguish between liberal
democratic states committed to popular government and individual
liberty, and totalitarian regimes based on rigid ideology wherein individual freedom is severely restricted and the few control the
many. Little wonder, then, that we have linked the open society
with democracy, so much so that the two are almost synonymous.
Taken together, they serve to conjure up the values, institutions,
processes, and ways of life that not only distinguish the "good"
regimes from the "bad," but also identify that which we should
cherish, cultivate, and defend against hostile forces both domestic
and foreign.

That Popper also intended to picture the open society in these
terms is, I think, evident from his discussion of its roots. He writes
of the "Great Generation. . . which lived in Athens just before, and
during the Peloponnesian war," of a generation that included
Pericles who, more clearly than others, perceived "that democracy
cannot be exhausted by the meaningless principle 'the people
should rule,' but that it must be based on faith in reason, and
humanitarianism." And, in Pericles' funeral oration, Popper
discerns other aspects of the open society which amount to a way of
life: merit, not social status or riches, should serve as the basis for
reward by the state ("When a citizen distinguishes himself, then he
will be called to serve the state, in preference to others, not as a
matter of privilege, but as a reward of merit; and poverty is no
bar"); due deliberation (discussion is not "a stumbling block in the
way of political action, but. . . an indispensable preliminary to acting wisely"); openness to the outside world ("Our city is thrown
open to the world; we never expel a foreigner"); active citizenship
("We consider a man who takes no interest in the state not as
harmless, but as useless"); humanitarianism ("We are taught. . .
never to forget that we must protect the injured"); individual
freedom ("we are not suspicious of one another, and do not nag our
neighbor if he chooses to go his own way"); happiness and bravery
("We believe that happiness is the fruit of freedom and freedom
that of valor, and we do not shrink from the dangers of war"); and
equal justice before the laws for all citizens, regardless of their
status ("The laws afford equal justice to all alike in their private
disputes").[4]

Clearly, the main characteristics of Popper's open society are
those we readily associate with the practices or aspirations of

modern liberal democracies; at this level, Popper's conception is unexceptional. Moreover, to a large extent, he slides over certain difficult and perennial problems inherent to liberal democracy such as those which center on the permissible limits of individual freedom in the social context. He seems content, that is, to provide the reader with a broad picture of the open society in order to highlight its essential features, particularly those which distinguish it from the closed society. Nevertheless, Popper's theory is highly controversial for reasons that are not difficult to discern. Not the least of these is his interpretation of Plato's works rendering Plato the father of the closed society. However, if we focus on his open society per se – that is, leave to one side his questionable interpretations – the most controversial aspects of his theory would seem to revolve, in one fashion or another, around what might be regarded as its "animating" principles, most notably critical rationalism, individual freedom, and toleration. To see this, let us begin by briefly examining Popper's depictions of the open and closed societies.

In Popper's view, the "humanitarian and rational theory of the state" which emerged from the period of the "Great Generation" can best be understood as an attack on the closed society, the assumptions and doctrines of which, Popper holds, were later systematically advanced in Plato's *Republic*. This theory, as interpreted by Popper, does not ask or attempt to answer "essentialist" questions relating to the nature or meaning of the state; nor does it concern itself with the "historicist" questions surrounding the whys and wherefores of the state's origins. Rather, in his words, it is concerned with another set of questions: "What do we demand from the state? What do we propose to consider as the legitimate aim of the state activity?" And in order to find out what our fundamental political demands are, we may ask: "Why do we prefer living in a well-ordered state to living without a state, i.e., in anarchy?" Popper regards these questions, in contrast to those of the essentialist or historicist, as "rational" in the sense that an individual must know what he wants "before he can proceed to the construction or reconstruction of any political institution."[5]

The reply of the humanists to these questions, according to Popper, is not hard to come by: "What I demand from the state," the humanist would say, "is protection; not only for myself, but for others too. I demand protection for my own freedom and for other people's. I do not wish to live at the mercy of anybody who has the

larger fists or the bigger guns. In other words, I wish to be protected against aggression from other men." The humanist, Popper
believes, would recognize that to achieve this end might well lead to
a limited curtailment of his own freedom of action by the state; a
realization, he holds, that in no way obscures the primary end of
the state which is to insure "the protection of that freedom which
does not harm other citizens." Moreover, in achieving this end, the
humanist, in Popper's words, would insist that "the state. . . limit
the freedom of citizens as equally as possible, and not beyond what
is necessary for achieving an equal limitation on freedom."[6]

Popper labels this the "protectionist theory of the state," though
he is quick to add that it should not be equated with a policy of non-
intervention or what libertarians might call the "night watchman"
state. For example, his theory would not foreclose a "certain
amount of state control in education" because, he reasons, the
youth need "to be protected from a neglect which would make them
unable to defend their freedom." Moreover, consonant with the
underlying values of this theory, there is a need for the state to insure "that all educational facilities are available to everybody." In
this vein, Popper is content to note that the protectionist theory
does not offer a cut-and-dried formula concerning the proper
boundaries between the individual and state domains of authority.
Nor does it seem that Popper is very much interested in exploring
this question because, from his vantage point, the chief virtue of his
protectionist theory is the absence of "any elements of historicism
or essentialism." "It does not say," he writes,

> that the state originated as an association of individuals with a pro-
> tectionist aim, or that any actual state in history was ever consciously
> ruled in accordance with this aim. And it says nothing about the
> essential nature of the state, nor about a natural right to freedom.
> Nor does it say anything about the way in which states actually func-
> tion.

What it does embody, Popper emphasizes, is a "political *demand*, or
more precisely, a proposal for the adoption of a certain policy."
And, he continues, only when formulated in terms of a demand or
proposal can the "social technologist. . . approach problems ra-
tionally, i.e. from the point of view of a fairly clear and definite
aim."[7]

This rationalism is integral to Popper's open society. While he does not discuss it in great detail – again, he seems intent on painting the large picture – he is clear enough concerning its essential character. The rationalist attitude (or the "attitude of reasonableness") is fundamentally one "of admitting 'I may be wrong and you may be right, and by an effort, we may get nearer to the truth.' " Bound up with this notion, Popper contends, are others which are intimately related to the fundamental character and principles of the open society. In the first place, there is an implied recognition in the rationalist attitude that any individual is "liable to make mistakes" that can be discovered "by others, or by himself with the assistance or the criticism of others." This suggests that an individual ought not "to be his own judge" as well as "the idea of impartiality." And, because "faith in reason is not only a faith in our own reason, but also – and even more – in that of others," even an individual who regards himself as intellectually superior to others cannot help but realize that "he is capable of learning from criticism as well as from his own and other people's mistakes." But this presupposes that one "takes others and their arguments seriously," which, in turn, is "bound up with the idea that the other fellow has a right to be heard, and to defend his arguments." By implication this leads to "the recognition of the claim to tolerance, at least of all those who are not intolerant themselves." Moreover, Popper sees a linkage between the idea of impartiality and that of responsibility: "we have not only to listen to arguments, but we have a duty to respond, to answer, where our actions affect others." From his perspective, then, rationalism requires "social institutions to protect freedom of criticism, freedom of thought, and thus the freedom of men."[8]

The closed society, of course, presents us with an almost entirely different picture. In this respect, Popper finds the chief elements of the closed society embedded in the tribalism of the ancient Greeks. In his view, the "magical attitude toward social custom" left little room for individual choice because the resulting taboos did not leave many loopholes and the right way was determined "by taboos, by magical tribal institutions" that were sacrosanct. As a consequence, change was infrequent and, in Popper's opinion, characterized by "religious conversions or revulsions or of the introduction of new magical taboos," not through rational efforts designed "to improve social conditions." What is more, the tribes were not only static but "dead" as well: their organic nature, fueled by the "group spirit of tribalism," rendered them virtually immune from the "strain of civilization" or the competition between individuals and interests so necessary for broadening the horizons of human existence.[9]

The tribal tendencies are, in Popper's interpretation, reflected in Plato's philosophy. Of Plato, he writes:

> Never was a man more in earnest in his hostility towards the individual. And this hatred is deeply rooted in the fundamental dualism of Plato's philosophy; he hated the individual and his freedom just as he hated the varying particular experiences, the variety of the changing world of sensible things. In the field of politics, the individual is to Plato the Evil One himself.[10]

Plato, in Popper's view, yearned for a unified, harmonious, organic state which could restore the "unity of tribal life." In his emphasis on holism, Popper argues, Plato advanced a collectivist, tribal, totalitarian conception of justice and morality, namely, that the interest of the group, tribe, or state is the criterion of good.[11]

Popper says a great deal more about the closed society in his interpretations and analyses of Hegel, Marx, Whitehead, and other modern historians and philosophers. What we see, he contends, is that the modern friends and exponents of the closed society are those who revive, in one fashion or another, the ideals of the closed society found in tribalism and Plato's philosophy. For instance, he regards Hegelianism as "the renaissance of tribalism." To this point, he writes:

> The historical significance of Hegel may be seen in the fact that he represents the 'missing link,' as it were, between Plato and the modern form of totalitarianism. Most of the modern totalitarians are quite unaware that their ideas can be traced back to Plato. But many know of their indebtedness to Hegel, and all of them have been brought up in the close atmosphere of Hegelianism.[12]

Thus, on Popper's showing, a study of ancient Greek tribalism and Plato's philosophy pretty much reveals the enduring ideals, values, and goals associated with a closed society.

With the basic characteristics and differences between Popper's open and closed societies before us, it is not difficult to appreciate why Popper's open society has come under attack. We can, perhaps, best begin with his critical rationalism, which is central to his open society, and work our way outward to the central concerns it raises.

Now the first thing to note about his rationalism is that it simultaneously serves to close and open a society. Though Popper, understandably enough, does not stress the restrictive side of his rationalism, it is nevertheless true that the ideal open society – a society, that is, committed to critical rationalism as he describes it – would be closed to revelation as a source of Truth. To put this otherwise, it is difficult to see how any revealed truth that is not amenable to the processes of critical rationalism could enjoy a status above that which he accords myths, taboos, and superstition. Indeed, what seems clear from Popper's discussion is that his critical rationalism has no room for Truth, period; that is, the process of give and take which he describes may edge us by slow degrees closer and closer to Truth over time, but we can never presume to be in possession of capital "T" truth, only small "t" truth. This asymptotic approach to the whole question of truth is characteristic of the relativism which pervades Popper's analysis.[13]

The openness which rationalism provides stems from this relativism. The accepted norms, values, mores, and customs of the open society are fit objects for the processes of critical rationalism; that is, both their substance and status are open to change or modification in a never-ending search for truth. On this score, the open society can never rest; at no point can its members ever uncritically subscribe to any belief, doctrine, or practice as embodying the "right" way. Indeed, the citizens of the open society should take it upon themselves to apply critical reason to the prevailing mores, institutions, and standards of society. What is more, each citizen is obliged to show toleration for those who do bring reason to bear on these matters – a *genuine* toleration, we must assume, which obliges the citizen to consider and weigh the pros and cons of all proposals for change with a truly open mind. This aspect of critical rationalism, as we shall see shortly, causes some difficulties.

This state of affairs, Popper acknowledges, creates an uneasiness and strain. In this connection, he believes that Plato's deep-seated animus toward the open society cannot be fully comprehended without realizing the enormous strain he was under due to the abrupt and almost total movement from the closed to the open society during the relatively short "Great Generation" period. Popper likens the strain of which he writes to that which children feel after a serious family quarrel or the breaking up of the family home; that is, the feeling of security is lost. But in even less turbulent times, he admits, the uneasiness and tensions are still very much with us: the "endeavor to be rational" forces individuals to look after themselves, to accept responsibilities, and to forgo at least some of their emotional social needs.[14]

Popper certainly seems to be aware of at least potential sources of unhappiness which inhere in the open society. He writes that with the loss of its "organic character, an open society may become, by degrees," what he terms an "abstract society." It may move, that is, towards a "completely abstract or depersonalized society" or one which, to a considerable extent, loses "the character of a concrete group of men, or of a system of such concrete groups." Such a society, as he describes it, is one "in which men practically never meet face to face – in which all business is conducted by individuals in isolation who communicate by typed letter or by telegrams, and who go about in closed motor car." He finds it "interesting. . . that our modern society resembles in many of its aspects such a completely abstract society." He concedes that "we do not always drive alone in closed motor cars (but meet face to face thousands of men walking past us in the street)"; but "the upshot," he feels, "is very nearly the same as if we did – we do not establish as a rule any personal relation with our fellow pedestrians." Popper also concedes that "there are many people living in a modern society who have no, or extremely few, intimate personal contacts, who live in anonymity and isolation, and consequently in unhappiness." This unhappiness he attributes to the fact that while "society has become abstract, the biological make-up of man has not changed much; men have social needs which they cannot satisfy in an open [abstract?] society."[15]

Popper holds that "a completely abstract or even a predominantly abstract society" is no more possible "than a completely rational or even a predominantly rational society." Why so? Because, in addition to the biological factor to which he refers, he believes men will "try to satisfy their emotional needs as well as they can" by forming "concrete groups and concrete social contacts of all kinds." Nevertheless, he is frank in recognizing that "most of the concrete social groups of a modern open society (with the exception of some lucky family groups) are poor substitutes, since they do not provide for a common life."[16] But, be that as it may, it would appear that Popper's answer to the basic concern regarding the capacity of a society committed to secular rationalism to cohere would take something like the following form: Man's natural or inherent needs – i.e., non-rational and even irrational "forces" – serve to harness the centripetal tendencies of the open society to a degree sufficient to prevent it from lapsing into a mere conglomeration of individuals.

Popper, we may say, evidences a concern about whether a society in which critical rationalism is exalted can long cohere; whether it can provide for the distinctly human needs, spiritual and emotional, which also bind and hold the society together. But his answer is hardly satisfactory because it raises problems which he seems to ignore or pass over. For instance, the concrete groups which come closest to fulfilling human needs would seem to weaken the communal ties which, to the extent they are based on critical rationalism, must necessarily be very fragile to begin with. Moreover, this strain could only intensify with a proliferation of such concrete groups so that, at the theoretical level at least, we are confronted with an apparent paradox: the more open the society, the greater the need for those groups which can provide friendship, a sense of belonging, stability, and a feeling of security.

Perhaps Popper is not concerned about such difficulties because he thinks that the proper degree of openness in a society will come about naturally once critical rationalism takes hold. It might be that the paramount problem from his point of view is insuring that critical rationalism takes hold because he believes the human needs will find some degree of fulfillment. Or to put this in somewhat stronger terms: Popper seems to hold that human emotions can extinguish critical rationalism, but critical rationalism can never extinguish human emotions. Thus, if this be his view of the matter, a society may be completely closed but never totally abstract.

No matter how we interpret Popper on this matter, however, his open society is clearly one in perpetual flux and highly vulnerable to potential danger. As we have already remarked, critical rationalism in Popper's theory is a force which knows no bounds. "In my opinion," he writes, "the only way in which excessive rationalism is likely to prove harmful is that it tends to undermine its own position and thus to further an irrationalist reaction."[17] The potential danger arises because the most likely targets of this rationalism are the beliefs, associations, institutions, or ways of life which at least partially satisfy felt human needs and emotions and serve as well to prevent the modern open society from descending into abstractness. Thus, metaphorically speaking, we are reasonably sure that in the open society at least some human needs and emotions can never be assured of finding a permanent home; they will be forced to wander from one shelter to another – many of them, to be sure, hastily constructed – as critical rationalism continues its relentless process of search and destroy.

Viewed from this perspective, Popper's work, in an important sense, represents not so much an attack on the closed society but rather on the Ancients' conception of the polis and its needs. One of their major concerns, and one which Popper either disparages or slides over, centered on the need for the cultivation and preservation of a high degree of oneness in the polis – a oneness which required a commonality, i.e., shared values, goals, and ways of life. For this reason, the "do your own thing" morality which seems so congenial to the guiding principles of the open society was anathema to them.

Popper's attitude is understandable. The modern liberal state, the context in which he writes, is far less holistic than the Greek polis; we now live with bifurcations between church and state or state and society which are completely foreign to the Ancients' conceptions of the polis. Yet, we are still left to wonder about the feasibility and desirability of Popper's open society. Our modern liberal societies are highly pluralistic and diverse, and, if there be any basis at all to the Ancients' concern, to haul into the processes of critical rationalism that which serves to provide some degree of cohesion and unity might well be to court disaster, not only for the society but for the individuals who comprise it as well. In any event, a crucial question that emerges from an analysis of the theory of the open society from this perspective is, How open can a society be and still be a society? – a decent and orderly society, that is.

To ask such a question brings us to the heart of a bitter and ongoing controversy – one which embraces a wide range of social and political issues. What is not contested is where to look in order to find evidence one way or the other, namely, to the United States. In his "Preface" to a revised edition of his open society volumes dated 1950, Popper writes that a recent visit to the United States buoyed his sagging hopes for the ideals of the open society. In this connection, he remarks about "a movement which began three centuries ago" which he describes as "perhaps the greatest of all moral and spiritual revolutions of history." He pictures this revolution as "the longing of uncounted unknown men to free themselves and their minds from the tutelage of authority and prejudice" and as an

> attempt to build up an open society which rejects the absolute authority of the merely established and merely traditional while trying to preserve, to develop, and to establish traditions, old or new, that measure up to its standards of freedom, of humaneness, and of rational criticism."[18]

Writing some twenty years late, Malcolm Muggeridge presents a totally different picture of the United States and Western civilization in general. For over a century, he argues, the "liberal mind" (one unmistakably influenced by the principles and ideals of the open society as Popper describes them) has "systematically, stage by stage," dismantled

> our Western way of life, depreciating and deprecating all its values so that the whole social structure is now tumbling down, dethroning its God, undermining all its certainties, and finally mobilizing a Praetorian Guard of ribald students, maintained at the public expense, and ready at the drop of a hat to go into action, not only against any institution or organ of the maintenance of law and order still capable of functioning, especially the police. And all this, wonderfully enough, in the name of health, wealth and happiness of all mankind.[19]

In terms of our previous analysis, it is fair to say that Muggeridge views the critical rationalism of the open society as leading to the dissolution of Western civilization by leaving the individual with precious little to cling to in terms of certainties and time-honored values.

While many might regard Muggeridge's indictment of the liberal mind as too harsh, there is no gainsaying his general point: individual freedom, critical rationalism along with relativism – the principle elements of Popper's open society theory – have served to

depreciate and devalue central values and ways of life in our society and those of other "free" nations as well, particularly since
World War II. We certainly do not lack examples to illustrate this
point. The nuclear family, long regarded as the basic unit of
Western societies, has been seriously undermined over the last
three decades by changing attitudes towards marriage, divorce,
premarital sex, and, among other things, birth out of wedlock.
Whereas thirty years ago there was, by all evidences, a consensus
about how to define a family, today this is a matter of some controversy. Abortion, now primarily resorted to as a means of birth
control, has come to be regarded as a "constitutional right," a fact
which reflects an enormous and fundamental shift on the part of a
large segment of the society concerning the most basic questions of
all, the meaning and purpose of human life. At another level, and
quite in keeping with the basic tenets of the open society, the scope
of constitutional protections for speech and press have been
broadened so far that scarcely any form of expression, symbolic or
otherwise, can be legally prohibited or punished. Child pornography, it is true, is now "off limits," but this only after the
members of the Supreme Court could find rationales for doing so
least offensive to the spirit of the open society.

Clearly, not all the woes that afflict the moral character of
American society can be laid at the doorstep of the open society
theory. Indeed, the proponents of this theory might well be the
first to point out that many of the alleged difficulties in our society
today to which Muggeridge alludes stem from the widespread acceptance of a modern natural rights theory whose tenets and
character hardly conform with those of the open society. For instance, the "rigidity" or inflexibility of the modern natural rights
theory, particularly with respect to the substance and character of
rights, contrasts sharply with the tentativeness associated with
critical rationalism. Nevertheless, it is perfectly clear that there is
an affinity between these theories because they both reject fundamental elements of the older natural law tradition and both are
wedded to broad ends such as securing a wide degree of individual
freedom. This insures a similarity of outlook with regard to those
issues that have produced the changes Muggeridge deplores.

Still another and more positive answer might take the following
form: While one might be hard pressed to defend all changes over,
say, the last forty years which have transformed American society,

the net effect of these changes has been beneficial. Today we find freer, more liberated and independent individuals – individuals more capable of exercising initiative and responsibility. To be sure, strain is associated with these changes; the society is now, perhaps, more abstract than it ever has been. But this strain is the price one must pay for the benefits of the open society. In this respect, Muggeridge can be compared to Plato; he yearns for a return to a much simpler age when moral and ethical standards were set from "above."

Yet, Muggerridge's charges – and those of many others who, for the sake of convenience, we may call "traditionalists" – cannot be so easily dismissed. Muggeridge's reference to "ribald students" brings forcefully to mind episodes of the late '60s and early '70s which justify, as perhaps no others possibly can, the traditionalist contentions relative to the character of the open society. I refer here to the student "rebellions" at many of our institutions of higher learning: rebellions which were frequently pictured in terms that would warm the heart of the most ardent enthusiast of the open society. Our universities, it was alleged, were but "tools" of the "establishment" which sought to rationalize and perpetuate an essentially corrupt social and political order. The functions of the universities, we might say, were regarded as something akin to those of the rituals, superstitions, myths, and taboos of tribalism; that is, in supporting the "establishment," they also sought to stifle critical inquiry into the foundations and structures of our social system.

I need not go into the details of this confrontation to note its irony: the presumed bastions of critical reason came under assault. In many cases individuals in the universities who had done their very best to foment discontent with our society and its ways – those who sought to "play" Socrates in their own small way – now found themselves under attack. Under these circumstances, we should have expected to see the open society principles, on a miniature scale at least, operating at their very best; after all, those under attack were well schooled in the need for and uses of critical reason, and they were situated in an environment conditioned more than any other in society to embrace reason. Beyond this, the attackers, taken as a whole, represented the more articulate and better educated of the young adults in society. Thus, we had every reason to expect that they would not be totally unaware of the demands of critical rationalism, the more so given their commitment to higher education.

But alas, this was not the case. To say that we did not see the open society at its best would be a gross understatement. What we did see was the closing of some schools and, in many cases, capitulation to the demands of the student protestors – demands which were hardly the outgrowth of processes associated with critical rationalism. Indeed, today many schools are still trying to undo changes which have served to weaken the curriculum and lower academic standards.

The reason most frequently advanced for the failure to achieve anything resembling the kind of exchange of views which is supposed to characterize the open society seems reasonable enough: namely, the student leaders of these protests and demonstrations used tactics which caused disruptions and, in some cases, violence. Thus, it was thought best to avoid confrontation even if this meant permanently damaging relationships within the university communities. But why, we must ask, the unwillingness to face up to the protestors when they had, by any conceivable standards, violated the rules required for reasonable discourse? And why the willingness to close down and/or capitulate when, by all evidence, the larger society would have readily backed the use of authority to restore order?

To the extent that actions or, in this case, inaction can be attributed to theoretical concerns – and here there is every reason to believe theory did play an extremely important role – the following observations seem relevant. Consider, to begin with, that questions concerning what universities should or should not be, while certainly legitimate, can only be answered by reference to higher, overarching values and goals. These values, in turn, bear a corresponding relationship to others so that, off at the end, to answer the original questions concerning the role of universities depends upon a more comprehensive view of the nature, purpose or ends of society. This realization alone renders it unlikely that proponents of the open society doctrines would say to the student protestors: "We have listened to what you have to say and to your demands which, after due deliberation, we reject. Now cease and desist and let the business of education proceed. Otherwise, we will be compelled to use legal force to expel you from university grounds." Why the improbability of such a stance? Because, more likely than not, open society advocates suffer from the "Socratic syndrome"; that is, they indiscriminately accept J.S. Mill's proposition that "All silencing of discussion is an assumption of infallibility," along with his stern warning, "Mankind can hardly be too often reminded, that there was once a man named Socrates."[20] Beyond this, the issue at hand, as we have seen, transcends the university and its role. This much at least was understood by the protestors. At stake, then, to some degree, were competing visions of the "good" society, and to have rejected the protestors' vision or visions would have been tantamount to claiming a kind of knowledge that devotees of the open society are loath to claim – i.e., a knowledge, however partial, of the good derived from values independent of those inherent in the open society theory.

This leads us to one of the traditionalist's basic concerns. As we have taken pains to note, the doctrine of the open society encourages subjecting society's ways of life, values, and institutions to critical rationalism. Leaving to one side the motives of those who engage in this process, it is not difficult to see how it can eventually lead to a "dismantling" of society in the sense suggested by Muggeridge. The basic reason for this would seem to be that, whereas critical rationalism may very well be suited for laying bare the inner workings and structures of institutions for all to see, it is scarcely of any help in reassembling them. The theory of the open society, as we have just seen, could be used to provide an excellent justification for the students' protests; yet, when affairs did get out of hand, its inherent values generated a paralysis. They could provide no goals, standards, principles that might serve as guides for a rational determination of the legitimate role of the university within the broader social context. They simply had no "hooks" to grapple with the situation. Moreover, the standards that were applied by those who sought to preserve the integrity of the universities against student agitators were drawn from a tradition whose abiding values are largely extraneous to those of the open society.

This situation points to a more general difficulty with the open society theory. The critical rationalists, ever vigilant to uphold the standards of the open society (i.e., "freedom," "humaneness," "critical reason"), frequently find themselves in the position of challenging the values, processes, norms, institutions, or traditions of society that do not meet these standards. Part of this challenging process, naturally enough, involves setting forth alternatives

with the end in mind of promoting critical rationalism and collective or individual freedom. And, judging from our experiences, we
know that these alternatives in many instances do become matters
of considerable controversy, particularly as they relate to social
values, norms, and lifestyles that "rub" a significant portion of the
community "the wrong way." In most cases, the controversy only
agitates the community. However, the issue in dispute can involve
deeply held values, in which case the controversy can become so intense as to cause widespread civil disorder. At the extreme the
very existence of society might itself be endangered.

Now according to the canons of the open society theory, a spirit
of "toleration" should prevail among the contending parties, at
least to a degree sufficient to prevent violent civil strife. Indeed,
ideally speaking, we may assume that toleration should serve to
ameliorate conflicts both great and small. But we know from experience and our knowledge of human nature that toleration cannot play the role assigned to it. For it to do so, moreover, would require a kind and degree of social control and indoctrination totally
foreign to the precepts of the open society. In this we see at least
one "natural" limitation to the realization of the ideal open society
in this world. But there is a normative dimension to this matter as
well. Presume that we could wave a magic wand so that toleration
would operate in the fashion envisioned in theory. Would this be a
desirable state of affairs? In some cases, no doubt. But, I think, one
would be hard pressed to argue that toleration *should* be the paramount value in all cases. Surely we can envision instances when to
do so would mean the abandonment of more deeply held values,
both individual and social. Put otherwise, unless we are prepared to
enshrine toleration – combined, of course, with critical rationalism – as the *summum bonum* of society, then our commitment
to the principles of the open society must be conditional.

This conclusion should not be taken to mean that a high value
should not be placed on individual freedom, critical rationalism,
and toleration. Most societies in the Western tradition value these
principles very highly as means to higher ends. Rather, what the
foregoing seems to indicate is that the application of these principles is necessarily conditioned by the traditions, norms, and
values which form the nucleus of the social fabric. Put otherwise,
these nuclear norms and values provide guides and standards for
the exercise of open society principles which, taken by themselves,

are far from self-executing; for example, they do not tell us much about the rules that should govern in the give and take necessary for critical rationalism. In fact, a strong case can be made that the notion of an open society derives both its attractiveness and plausibility from the manner in which its principles have been shaped consonant with more basic traditional values.

In these terms the problems surrounding the open society would seem to stem from its principles (a) being abstracted from the context in which they grew and developed, and then; after having been so abstracted, (b) set up as goals without regard to the social context from which they were derived. Both these developments are disturbing but it is (b) which creates tensions; it serves to turn these principles against the traditions and values that gave them birth and meaning. It leads to the kind of dismantling to which Muggeridge referred.

Will this tension eventually lead to the dissolution of society? The answer to this question, in my judgment, depends on how one defines society. If, for instance, we think of society in terms that Cicero conceived of a "Commonwealth," then we are bound to see a dissolution. For him a Commonwealth was "not any collection of human beings brought together in any sort of way." Rather it was "an assemblage of people in large numbers associated in agreement with respect to justice and a partnership for the common good." "For what," he asked rhetorically, "is a state except an association or partnership in justice?"[21] If, on the other hand, the society is, as many modern behaviorists would have it, simply a collection of individuals who interact with one another under a common political authority, then it is likely to survive. In other words, the most fertile grounds for the open society would seem to be a "minimal" society, one in which individuals are loosely conjoined with few common ends. Openness, in other words, carries with it a high price.

Notes

[1] Karl R. Popper, *The Open Society and Its Enemies*, 1st ed. rev. (Princeton: Princeton University Press, 1950). I am not in substantial disagreement with Professor Berns (see his "Re-evaluating the Open Society") in saying this. My concern is not with Popper's interpretation of Plato. Nor would I argue that Popper's work is not largely forgotten, though this is a moot point. What I would argue is that we find in this work the principles which undergird the concept of the open society. To put this in other terms, it is the best source for locating the foundations of the theory of the open society.

[2] Henri Bergson, *The Two Sources of Morality and Religion* (New York: Henry Holt and Co., 1935).

[3] See Dante Germino's "Democracy and the Open Society" in this volume. Also see his "Henri Bergson: Activist Mysticism and the Open Society," *Political Science Reviewer* 9 (1979).

[4] Popper, op. cit., 181-82.

[5] Ibid., 108.

[6] Ibid., 108-9.

[7] Ibid., 110-11.

[8] Ibid., 423-24.

[9] Ibid., 168.

[10] Ibid., 103.

[11] Ibid., 106.

[12] Ibid., 226.

[13] On this point see Willmoore Kendall, "The 'Open Society' and Its Fallacies," *American Political Science Review* 54 (December, 1960).

[14] Popper, op. cit., 172.

[15] Ibid., 170.

[16] Ibid., 170-71.

[17] Ibid., 415.

[18] Ibid., viii.

[19] Malcolm Muggeridge, "The Death Wish," *Human Life Review* 10 (Summer 1984). Reprinted from *Esquire* (December, 1970).

[20] John Stuart Mill, *Utilitarianism, Liberty, and Representative Government* (New York: E.P. Dutton and Co., 1950), 113.

[21] Cicero, *On the Commonwealth*, i. 25.

Re-evaluating the Open Society

Walter Berns

In a volume devoted to a reconsideration of the open society issue, it is very tempting to devote a good deal of attention to Karl Popper's book, *The Open Society and Its Enemies.*[1] It is such an easy target. Popper devotes page after page, chapter after chapter, to a denunciation of Plato, whom he sees as the open society's greatest enemy, and whom he misunderstands. What he has to say about Plato is, in my judgment, ludicrous.

One could readily demonstrate this, but there is little purpose in doing so. Besides, Popper himself might reply as Robert Benchley once replied to his critics. Benchley, who was a very funny man and also, for a while, a newspaper columnist, once finished a column – on late bloomers, probably – with the statement, "after all, Mozart didn't write his last symphony until he was 56." As you might expect, this brought him a deluge of mail pointing out that Mozart died in his thirty-fifth year. Unperturbed, Benchley, in a subsequent column, replied that he didn't know what Mozart his correspondents were referring to; he was referring to Leon Mozart who used to live above Zabar's delicatessen at Broadway and 81st Street and who could still be found up in the Catskills playing the piano at Grossinger's.

So I think I shall ignore Popper's book. It is one of those modern volumes that is both largely forgotten and deserves to be. Having said this, I must immediately admit to being prejudiced in favor of older books. In my own field, which I would describe as constitutional government or constitutionalism, the new books seem to have forgotten not only the answers to the important questions but the questions themselves.

I take this particular formulation from a relatively new and good book, *Remembering the Answers*,[2] in which Nathan Glazer points out that in the '60s, in the university (the proudest symbol of the open society), and beginning at Berkeley, the students began to ask questions that had not been asked in generations and to which faculty and administration alike had forgotten the answers: Why, for a banal example, should students be required to wear shoes in the dining halls? And, more significantly, should students not be granted an equal share of the governing of the university? And, still more significantly, why shouldn't the university, which, after all, had become the multiversity, be made over into a community, a participatory democracy? And, finally, why should not constitutional government as we have known it in the United States be refashioned into a participatory democracy?

With this question a whole generation of intellectuals was sent back to Rousseau, from which this idea of participatory democracy derived, and more precisely to the romantic Rousseau who attacked the open society, who advocated censorship in the course of denouncing the arts and sciences (the hallmarks of the open society), and who praised the simple, self-reliant, bare-footed, family-oriented and, if not guitar-strumming, then at least psalm-singing villagers of Neufchatel, the closed and simple society. Their work began to fill the professional journals. In this return to Rousseau, however, in their quest for the closed society, they overlooked the scientist Rousseau, the artist Rousseau, the Rousseau who, knowing that he himself could not live in any sort of closed society, and especially not Neufchatel, wrote *The Dreams of a Solitary Walker*.

It is not only the student rebels of the '60s, or the middle-aged *enfants terribles* of the New Left, who have begun to have misgivings concerning the open society. So, in their own way, have the so-called Moral Majority who, for example, would return "creationism"–itself, however, a neologism–to the public school curriculum. And so have we professors, and nothing would be more helpful to us as we attempt a reconsideration of the open society than an explication of Rousseau's works. All of them. It was Rousseau the philosopher who first broke with philosophy and with Hobbes and Locke, the political founders of the open society. And it was Rousseau who astonished his philosophic friends by attacking the Enlightenment and the entire project that modern philosophy had launched. Allan Bloom, in the introduction to his translation of Rousseau's letter to d'Alembert on the theater, has described this project as follows:

> Philosophy would purge men of prejudice and make their duties clear without the aid of superstition; the fine arts would civilize them and remove their barbarous rudeness, a vestige of earlier times; and the mechanical arts would procure them a longer and more comfortable life.[3]

His great contemporaries, Voltaire, d'Alembert, and the others, thought he was mad when he refused to join them in fostering this project, but with the benefit of hindsight we can see that Rousseau was, perhaps, very sane indeed, and quite prescient. Not in precise detail, of course, but in general outline he foresaw the consequences of this project: the Bomb, the crime rate, and the popular culture whose vulgarity cannot be concealed by Nielsen ratings.

But I must leave it to my philosophic colleagues to explicate Rousseau's thought on the open society. My competence lies elsewhere, in American constitutionalism, for example, a field that happens to offer a good deal of material that is relevant to our concerns. Indeed, the United States can be said to have emerged out of a debate between the advocates of the open society (we know them as Federalists) and the advocates of a more or less closed society (the Anti-Federalists), one of whom, Samuel Adams, hoped to build in Boston "the *Christian* Sparta,"[4] and the boggled imagination cannot picture a society more closed than a Christian Sparta. In what is probably the best statement of the grounds on which the Anti-Federalists opposed the Constitution, Mercy Warren, looking at the system of government that opened the country to the commerce, the luxury, and the ideas of the world, regretted that a fence had not been built "around her sea-board," and, instead of allowing Americans to extend their vision "over the boundless desert," regretted that "*a Chinese wall* had not been stretched along the Apalachian ridges." This, she added, "might have kept the nations [i.e., the states] within the boundaries of nature."[5] What better serves to symbolize the closed society than a society enclosed by a Chinese wall?

In the event, of course, the Anti-Federalists – who, in fact, were not nearly so old-fashioned as their rhetoric and metaphors would suggest – were strong enough, or numerous enough, to effect no more than a compromise: the states and their simpler societies were retained but they were comprised in a more perfect union designed to secure "the blessings of liberty." The Constitution of this union was founded on newly discovered scientific principles. The "openness" of the society that would be built under the aegis of this Constitution should have surprised no one, and it surely did not surprise Mercy Warren. The Constitution said nothing about a community in which citizens were bound to each other by duties; its purpose was to secure rights. True, the only right specifically mentioned in the original, unamended Constitution is the right of authors and inventors to their respective writings and discoveries, a right Congress was empowered to secure, this in order "to promote the progress of science and useful arts."[6] But what better serves to symbolize the open society than a constitutional provision that ties the country to science and its discoveries? The United States was to be a *novus ordo seclorum*, a motto proclaimed on its great seal which, in turn, is displayed on every dollar bill; in its devotion to the modern project, it would be the home, in Shelley's phrase, of *Prometheus Unbound*:

> The loathsome mask has fallen, the man remains
> Sceptreless, free, uncircumscribed, but man
> Equal, unclassed, tribeless and nationless.[7]

Unkinder poets have denominated this unclassed, tribeless, and nationless – or open – society, the universal homogeneous state, the state inhabited by Nietzsche's "last men"[8] and deplored by anyone who respects the human community, or better, the community of truly human beings. The most profound of the Anti-Federalists – Mercy Warren again comes to mind – had some notion of where Prometheus might lead them.

I am suggesting that the tensions between the principles of the open and closed societies are, to a degree, built into the American federal system. It was John Marshall, the Federalist, who, in the course of upholding Congress's power to charter a national bank, spoke of a "vast republic, from the St. Croix to the Gulf of Mexico, from the Atlantic to the Pacific [in which] revenue is to be collected and expended [and across which] armies are to be marched and supported."[9] And it was Luther Martin, refusing to sign the Constitution and urging his state of Maryland not to ratify it, who argued the case against Congress's power and in favor of the state's power to remain a financial, and thereby, he hoped, a cultural community unto itself. The United States prevailed in that dispute; the country is, and has long been, one large commercial republic in which citizens are related to each other, if at all, by the business contracts they enter into. But the states, until recently at least, prevailed in other areas, areas, it might be said, where are to be found the institutions of a closed society, where citizens are joined in families and other primary associations. For example, although I suspect the rule of the case is no longer good law, it was as recently as 1956 that the Supreme Court said that "there is no federal law of domestic relations."[10] That being so, it was up to the states to decide whether an illegitimate child may inherit from the father. (Justice Douglas, as one might expect, refused to accept this.) One of the two questions the Court had to decide in this case was whether the term "children" in the federal copyright law includes an illegitimate child. "Strangely enough," Justice Harlan said in the opinion of the Court, "[that question has] never before been decided, although the statutory provisions involved have been part of the Act in their present form since 1870."[11] But there should have been nothing strange about this; decisions respecting such matters belonged to the states, not Congress and not the federal courts. John Marshall would have agreed with that, just as he would have agreed that, however open the society was to be in some respects, it was to be closed in others. Here, for example, is Marshall on the family and the dependence of the United States on the family:

> All know and feel, the plaintiff as well as others, the sacredness of the connection between husband and wife. All know that the sweetness of social intercourse, the harmony of society, the happiness of families depend on that mutual partiality which they feel, or that delicate forebearance which they manifest towards each other.[12]

This is not the sort of language that we would expect to find in an opinion of the contemporary Supreme Court; nor was it the sort of language Marshall would have employed had he been formed only by the political philosophy of the open society, the political philosophy underlying the Constitution. His jurisprudence did much to promote the large commercial republic where the worth of a man is his price, and the survival of an institution depends on its ability to turn a profit, but, as one of his biographers has noted, Marshall came to be aware of the tensions between the sort of person he admired and the jurisprudence he espoused. He seemed to have sensed a certain deterioration in the American character, "wondered about its cause," and wondered, too, about its political consequences.[13] A Lockean in his public philosophy, his private character had been formed in a pre-Lockean America, and he came to realize that a Lockean America could not survive if it were to become populated only by Lockeans. In a letter to John Randolph, written towards the end of his long life, Marshall lamented the passing of a generation guided by "venerable maxims" and characterized by "religious reverence," an age that took seriously the moral education of its young. How, he wondered, could republican virtue survive in a purely commercial society?[14] In saying this, Marshall, unknowingly, was reflecting Rousseau's insight that under the new dispensation the citizen was replaced by the bourgeois, the human type that, as Allan Bloom has noted, "when dealing with others, thinks only of himself, and on the other hand, in his understanding of himself, thinks only of others."[15] A product of the older and closed society, Marshall, like the other Founders of America, nevertheless dedicated his public life to the cause of the new and open society whose principles Americans learned from John Locke.

Nominally, Locke's purpose in writing his *Two Treatises* was to refute Filmer who, in his *Patriarcha*, had advanced the cause of the divine right of kings to rule by arguing that they were the direct heirs of Adam whose right to rule came from God. Whatever might be said of Filmer's argument, and Locke said most of it in his *First Treatise*, it was compatible with, even if it was not required by, the Christian teaching as to the law: "Thou shalt love the Lord thy God with all thy heart, and with all thy soul, and with all thy mind. This is the first and great commandment. And the second is like unto it; Thou shalt love thy neighbor as thyself."[16] Filmer's king ruled in the name of God, over subjects who were understood to be the children of God and, as such, were enjoined to love each other, and to assist each other; who were to be joined in holy matrimony, which (according to the old Book of Common Prayer) is an estate, "instituted of God, signifying . . . the mystical union that is betwixt Christ and his church"; and the children of such unions were enjoined to honor their fathers and mothers, just as their parents took a vow, registered in heaven, to love, comfort, and honor each other, and keep each other in times of sickness as well as of health.

Locke did more than refute Filmer's divine right argument; he found a new "rise of government, another original of political power," a new basis for political power. As Hobbes had argued before him, this proved to be a political power derived from the fact that by nature man is an *asocial* animal, living in a state of absolute freedom and equality, governed only by a law of nature that prescribes that he should preserve his own life and, "when his own preservation comes not in competition," preserve the rest of mankind.[17]

This is the origin of that principle on the basis of which we Americans would build our open society. A version of it appears in the Declaration of Independence where the point is made that all men are created equal insofar as they all possess the rights of life, liberty, and the pursuit of happiness, and that government is instituted "to secure these rights," these individual rights, these selfish rights. Instead of being all children of God, obligated to each other by commandments issued by God, men were seen to be governed only by a law that obliges them to take care of themselves – and take care of others only when it costs them nothing or at most little to do so.

One is bound to wonder if this is an accurate account of the human condition. Is there nothing in nature that binds one human being to another, even if, in so doing, it cuts him off (and those to whom he is bound) from the rest of the world? To state the question in its simplest form, is there nothing in nature that makes man a social animal?

The greatest challenge to Locke's understanding would seem to come from the family and the affection its members have for each other: husband for wife, wife for husband; parents for children, children for parents. That is to say, if there are bonds joining human beings – I mean bonds other than those forged in civil society and by the laws of civil society – or, stated otherwise, if man by nature is a social animal, this would show itself most evidently in generation and in the family. It is this challenge that Locke attempts to meet in chapter six of the *Second Treatise* ("Of Paternal

Power"), and in the opening sections, devoted to "conjugal society," of chapter seven.

What, according to Locke, is the nature of the associations that characterize the family? What, for example, is it that binds the male of the human species to the female? Here is Locke's answer: "And herein . . . lies the chief, if not the only, reason why the male and female in mankind are tied to a longer conjunction than other creatures, viz., because the female is capable of conceiving, and *de facto* is commonly with child again and brings forth, too, a new birth long before the former is out of a dependency for support on his parents' help and able to shift for himself and has all the assistance that is due to him from his parents; whereby the father, who is bound to take care for those he has begot, is under an obligation to continue in conjugal society with the same woman longer than other creatures whose young being able to subsist of themselves before the time of procreation returns again, the conjugal bond dissolves of itself, and they are at liberty, till Hymen at his usual anniversary season summons them again to choose new mates."[18]

The male stays with the female because of his duty to care for that which he begot. What, then, is the nature of that duty? It is, Locke says, a duty prescribed by "all the laws a man is under, whether natural or civil."[19] I know from the way Locke writes that this means that man is not under any divine law, which means he has no duty imposed by God to stay with the mother of his children. As for duties imposed by the civil laws, they vary from place to place. Where the civil laws permit a woman to have more than one husband at a time, Locke says, the duty of the father becomes altogether ambiguous.[20] Besides, the duties prescribed by the civil laws will depend ultimately on what are understood to be the laws by which the civil laws ought to be guided. As to these, Locke, as I say, mentions only the law of nature that commands each of us to take care of himself first, or, as he puts it in the *First Treatise*, nature requires that men should care for their children "after themselves."[21] Or, once again, that the father, "if it be necessary to *his* condition," may require his children to work "for their own subsistence."[22] By this, Locke means that the father's duty to care for the young is not really a duty.

And what of the obligations owed by children to their parents? They are compelled by their weakness when they are young to obey their parents; so the question becomes one of their obligations when they are grown. Locke says children are under a perpetual obligation to honor their parents (thus making it appear that he is presenting a traditional teaching), but he then adds, and repeats the addition later, "more or less, as the father's care, cost, and kindness in his education, have been more or less."[23] In this regard, it should be mentioned that, so far as I know, there is not *one* passage in the *Two Treatises* where Locke says that it is natural for children to love their parents, or to have anything resembling a natural affection for them. He is aware that grown children frequently obey their fathers and even show respect to them. How does he explain this? He explains it by the power fathers have to bestow their estates "on those who please them best." A father may bestow it "with a more sparing or liberal hand, according as the behavior of this or that child hath comported with his will and humor. This is no small tie on the obedience of children."[24] I can, perhaps, best convey an understanding of the purport of Locke's view of the family by quoting this passage:

> The nourishment and education of their children is a charge so incumbent on parents for their children's good that nothing can absolve them from taking care of it. And though the power of commanding and chastising them go along with it, yet God has woven into the principles of human nature such a tenderness for their offspring that there is little fear that parents should use their power with too much rigor; the excess is seldom on the severe side, the strong bias of nature drawing the other way. And therefore God Almighty, when he would express his gentle dealing with the Israelites, he tells them that, though he chastened them, "he chastened them as a man chastens his son.[25]

A parent's natural tenderness for his child is comparable to God's gentle treatment of the Israelites. How gentle or tender was that? Or, how gentle did Locke think it was? The Biblical quotation is from Deuteronomy 8:5, where we learn that God banished the Israelites to the wilderness for forty years and threatened to kill them if they disobeyed His commandments to worship Him. In short, in Locke's view, not at all gentle.

Locke's purpose in this chapter was to give an account of the relations between the members of the family that is fully compatible with his understanding of the natural condition of mankind. The

Second Treatise begins with the proposition that man is by nature asocial, governed by the law of self-preservation; the institution of the family suggests that by nature men are social; his account suggests that this sociality is merely conventional, and, except for the instinctive attachment of the mother to her child, not natural. In any case, the civil societies built on this presumed natural sociality were, in Locke's view, if not replicas of Hobbes's state of war, wherein the life of man was solitary, poor, nasty, brutish, and short, not free. They were not free to the extent they were closed societies squabbling with each other. Hence, rather than attempt to establish freedom on the basis of a presumed sociality, Locke would found it on self-interest. "The great and chief end. . . of men's uniting into commonwealths and putting themselves under government is the preservation of their property,"[26] by which Locke meant the property right, or the right to acquire.

Property is the subject of the chapter preceding the one on parents and children. Locke's teaching in that chapter is a complete denial of the traditional notion of man's obligations or duties respecting property; he teaches that the individual is free to accumulate as much as he pleases and to do with it as he sees fit. Locke's completely *emancipated* individual, acting only with a view to his self-interest, will so increase the wealth of nations, thereby solving the problem of scarcity – will so relieve man's estate on this earth – that the principal cause of civil disruptions will be removed and freedom will reign.

Other considerations went into the building of the Constitution of the United States, but the principles were Locke's. The United States was not to be a Christian commonwealth: Article VI forbids religious tests for office holders and the First Amendment forbids any law respecting an establishment of religion. The Constitution says nothing about the education of citizens, and the national government ignored the subject, more rather than less, until our own time. A government whose purpose is to secure private rights will be an apolitical government, an instrumental or administrative government, one that is limited, as Herbert Storing put it, to "facilitating the peaceful enjoyment of the private life."[27] It will take men as they are and let them alone. The first object of such a government, says Madison in the tenth *Federalist*, is the "protection of different and unequal faculties of acquiring property." What the governments of the various states would do, and be authorized to do, was another matter.

In the discussion of the family in America in his classic, *Democracy in America*, there appears a long and interesting footnote in which Tocqueville compares France and the United States with respect to what he calls political and civil legislation.[28] Political legislation – we would say, constitutional principles – was, he says, in the United States to a greater extent than in France, informed by modern principles; with respect to civil legislation, however, the opposite was true. This comment followed his observation that the Americans "have not yet thought fit to strip the parent, as has been done in France, of one of the chief elements of parental authority by depriving him of the power of disposing of his property at his death. In the United States there are no restrictions on the powers of a testator."

The civil legislation of the United States, in Tocqueville's sense of that term, was the responsibility of the state governments; this civil legislation included the law that was enforced in state courts, without, at that time, appeal to the Supreme Court of the United States. Almost everything having to do with the family, to the extent that it was affected by law, was governed by local law, both statutory and common. (The case to which I referred earlier and from which I quoted a statement of John Marshall's was decided in federal courts only because the case arose in the District of Columbia; it was not a "federal question" case in the sense of Article III of the Constitution.) This local law governing the family was a vestige of the law that predated not only the writing of the Constitution and the Declaration of Independence but, to a great extent, predated as well the discovery of those new political principles by John Locke (and, before him, Thomas Hobbes). By the common law, in force in most of the states, it was the duty of parents to support their minor children, and this was a duty founded on "the law of morality." Connecticut imposed this duty by statute, and the same statute made it a duty of grandparents to support their grandchildren, children their parents, and grandchildren their grandparents. Again, under the common law a father had a right of action against the man who, by "debauching" his daughter, brings disgrace upon the family. And, for a final example, the rule that a husband and wife cannot be witness for or against each other was grounded on the anxious solicitude of the law for domestic tranquility. Partly for the same reason (but "also, upon the ground, that the children of the marriage would be affected by it"), a wife was not allowed to "bastardize" her issue "by proving the non-access of her husband."[29]

Anyone concerned for the health of the family as an institution would have wanted to maintain the separation between "political legislation" and "civil legislation," between nation and state, between the new principles and the old practice. That old practice protected the family as the place of love; which means, it had to be constituted by erotic human beings, the sort of human beings who form communities and closed societies; the new principles derived from teachings – Locke's, preeminently – that are "notably unerotic." As Allan Bloom has put it, Locke is the least erotic of political philosophers. Lockean men are "calculating, fear-motivated. . . individuals, not directed towards others, towards couplings and the self-forgetting implied in them."[30] And for our purposes – our political purposes, I should make clear – this is what matters, this "self-forgetting," this capacity to care for another which produces a willingness to care for others. (The Beatles worried about this when they asked, "will you still need me, will you still feed me, when I'm 64?") It was Tocqueville's view that the health of the United States depended, in part, on the health of the family, and that the health of the family depended on women. If he were asked "to what the singular prosperity and growing strength of [the American] people ought mainly to be attributed, [he] should reply," he said, "to the superiority of their women."[31] He writes:

> No free communities ever existed without morals and. . . morals are the work of women. Consequently, whatever affects the condition of women, their habits and their opinions, has great political importance in my eyes.[32]

Women do this work as wives and mothers; they are equal to men, but their function is not the same as men's, and they must be educated to accept this function. A democratic education, Tocqueville says, "is indispensable to protect women from the dangers with which democratic institutions and manners surround them."[33] Without going into any detail, women must be educated to seek their happiness as wives and mothers.[34] (That this requires them to give up something – for example, sexual freedom – is the loudest complaint of our age.) Unlike the closed society, the open society is not the family writ large, but this does not make it independent of the moral training that the family provides – and must provide, if even the open society is to survive.

The bridging of the gap between political and civil legislation, nation and state, and open society and (somewhat) closed society, was accomplished by means of the Fourteenth Amendment. When, for example, Bruce Hafen points out that the "two traditions of individualism and family life [are] on a collision course,"[35] he refers to Supreme Court decisions having to do with abortion, testamentary dispositions, bastards, and obscenity, all resting on the Fourteenth Amendment. The Fourteenth Amendment has, for many legal scholars, become the Constitution, and it is by means of the Fourteenth Amendment that family law (or law affecting the family) is being nationalized or made part of our individualistic "political legislation."

In 1821, when questions of "civil legislation" were still understood to be matters of state and local law, the publisher of *Memoirs of a Woman of Pleasure*, otherwise known as *Fanny Hill*, was prosecuted, and convicted, in Massachusetts, and, when he appealed, the principle question was whether the trial court had acted properly when it refused to allow the jury to see a copy of the book. The Massachusetts Supreme Court upheld the trial court: to allow the book to be displayed upon the records of the court, said Chief Judge Parker, "would be to require that the public itself should give permanency and notoriety to indecency, in order to punish it."[36] And there the matter rested – for some 140 years. By the time *Fanny Hill* made its second appearance in the courts of Massachusetts, the freedom of the press had been made part of that liberty protected by the Fourteenth Amendment against restrictive state action, which meant that Massachusetts could not have the last word. That now belonged to the Supreme Court of the United States, and, as one might have expected, the Court ruled in favor of liberty – that is, in this case, pornography, whore's writing, and Fanny Hill was a whore.[37]

Individualism rests on liberty: the liberty to publish, the liberty to read, the liberty to "control one's own body," the liberty to do all those things that the law of the Fourteenth Amendment now protects; but the institution of the family rests on something other than liberty: on constraint, for example, on constraint assumed or accepted on behalf of others and enforced by the laws of the closed society. Of all the institutions of American society, the family is the least well adapted to definition in terms of the rights of its members, for to be given a right is to be given a claim against another. The institution of the family depends, in part, on the willingness of the husband and the wife to forgo "rights," e.g., the right to what has come to be called sexual freedom. Yet, one consequence of the Supreme Court's obscenity decisions has been what I have called the "publification" of sex, and that has had the result of making sexual gratification into the measure of existence. On this point, I am ashamed to say, I can do no better than to quote what I wrote five years ago:

> The ending of censorship brought out into the open an activity that had formerly, and for very good reasons, been confined to the private world. It emancipated sex, or so we are constantly being told; but not at all surprisingly, this emancipated sex turns out to be sex abstracted from its human setting. The immediate and obvious consequence of this is that sex is now being made into the measure of existence, and such uniquely human qualities as modesty, fidelity, abstinence, chastity, delicacy, and shame, qualities that formerly provided the constraints on sexual activity and the setting within which the erotic passion was enjoyed, discussed, and evaluated, are today ridiculed as merely arbitrary interferences "with the health of the sexual parts." Seemingly sober men and women, bearing the credentials of science, abstract from everything human to draw their picture of sexual man, the man seeking *The Joy of Sex* (whose author is quoted in the *New York Times* as telling us to re-examine fidelity with its "religio-social dogmas, personal feelings, fantasy needs, and the deeply proprietorial attitudes of one another enjoined on husband and wife by the priest, the neighbor, folklore and the attorney").[38]

I am not arguing that we can blame everything on the changes effected in the law by the Supreme Court. When Tocqueville wrote, men and women were busy; now they have time on their hands. Then, the imagination was confined; now, thanks to technology and popular culture, nothing limits it and everything excites it. But I would insist that it was the Supreme Court that made sex a public thing, and that it was this "publification" of sex that made it so easy for men and women – for husband and wife – to forget the vows they had taken to each other. In the past – in the America Tocqueville described, for example – public opinion censured, even condemned, shamelessness and infidelity, and especially shamelessness and infidelity on the part of the wife. But public opinion depends on law, as Lincoln taught us, on the support of the law, to the same extent that law depends on public opinion; change one, and the other will be changed. And the Supreme Court changed the law, with the result that what was once understood to be shameful is no longer so regarded. If a president, Jimmy Carter, and a leading conservative, William F. Buckley, may publish in *Playboy*, women, including married women, are surely entitled to comport themselves according to the standards laid down by *Playboy*. But those are standards that will destroy the family.

None of this was said in the obscenity litigation; the publishers of *Fanny Hill* could not afford to make this argument, and the state of Massachusetts had forgotten how to make it. The argument was implicit in the old law, but when the old law was challenged by the new principles, the old family by modern individualism, it turned out that no one could successfully defend the old. No one could provide an *argument* against "doing your own thing"; but a completely open society in which everyone does his own thing cannot survive. It would be not a divided house; it would not even be a house.

Notes

[1] Karl Popper, *The Open Society and Its Enemies*, 2 vols. (London: Routledge and Kegan Paul, 1945).

[2] Nathan Glazer, *Remembering the Answers: Essays on the American Student Revolt* (New York: Basic Books, 1970).

[3] Jean Jacques Rousseau, *Politics and the Arts: Letter to M. d'Alembert on the Theatre*, trans. Allan Bloom (Glencoe, Ill.: The Free Press, 1960), xvii.

[4] Samuel Adams, "Letter to John Scollay," December 30, 1780, in Harry Alonzo Cushing, ed., *The Writings of Samuel Adams*, 4 vols. (New York: G.P. Putnam's Sons, 1908) 4: 237-238.

[5] Mercy Warren, *History of the Rise, Progress and Termination of the American Revolution*, in Herbert J. Storing, ed., *The Complete Anti-Federalist*, 7 vols. (Chicago: University of Chicago Press, 1981) 6: 221.

[6] Article I, sec. 8, no. 8.

[7] Percy Bysshe Shelley, "Prometheus Unbound," III, iv, 193.

[8] See George Grant, *Technology and Empire: Perspectives on North America* (Toronto: House of Anasi, 1969), esp. ch. 1.

[9] McCulloch v. Maryland, 4 Wheat. 316, 408 (1819).

[10] De Sylva v. Ballentine, 351 U.S. 570, 580 (1956).

[11] Ibid., 572-3.

[12] Sexton v. Wheaton, 8 Wheat. 299, 239 (1823).

[13] Robert K. Faulkner, *The Jurisprudence of John Marshall* (Princeton: Princeton University Press, 1968), 135.

[14] Ibid., 136.

[15] Rousseau, *Emile or On Education*, trans. Allan Bloom (New York: Basic Books, 1979), 5.

[16] Matthew 22: 37-39.

[17] John Locke, *Treatises*, II, sec. 6.

[18] Ibid., sec. 80.

[19] Ibid., sec. 59.

[20] Ibid., sec. 65.

[21] Ibid., I, sec. 89.

[22] Ibid., II, sec. 65.

[23] Ibid., secs. 67, 70.

[24] Ibid., secs. 72-73.

[25] Ibid., sec. 67.

[26] Ibid., sec. 124.

[27]Herbert J. Storing, "American Statesmanship: Old and New," in Robert A. Goldwin, ed., *Bureaucrats, Policy Analysts, Statesmen: Who Leads?* (Washington, D.C.: American Enterprise Institute, 1980), 97.

[28] Alexis de Tocqueville, *Democracy in America*, 2 vols. (New York: Vintage Books, 1945), 2: 203.

[29]Tapping Reeve, *The Law of Baron and Femme*, 3rd ed. (Albany, N.Y., 1862), 412-414, 425, 292-295.

[30] Rousseau, *Emile*, 21.

[31] Tocqueville, *loc. cit.*, 225.

[32] Ibid., 209.

[33] Ibid., 211.

[34] Ibid., bk. 3, ch. 10.

[35] Bruce C. Hafen, "Puberty, Privacy, and Protection: The Risks of Children's Rights," *American Bar Association Journal* 63 (October 1977): 1384.

[36] Commonwealth v. Holmes, 17 Mass. 336 (1821).

[37] A Book. . . v. Att. General, 383 U.S. 413 (1966).

[38] Walter Berns, *The First Amendment and the Future of American Democracy* (New York: Basic Books, 1976), 221.

Law, Lawyers, and Property:
The Open Society and its Limitations

George Anastaplo

*In those days there was no king in Israel: every man did that which
was right in his own eyes.*

Judges 21:25

I chanced not long ago upon a radio preacher who had occasion to
say, in explicating a Biblical text, "We don't use 'prudent.' It's ar-
chaic – it has passed us by." And one of our youngsters recently
discovered in the course of a college seminar that she was the only
student in her class who knew the meaning of prudence. Yet, it
seems to me, the status and uses of "prudence" are matters vital to
any inquiry about a regime. Prudence is often regarded with suspicion. What precisely is considered wrong with prudence seems to
depend on the character of the particular regime. A tyranny is
wary of prudence because it calls such a regime into question by in-
sisting that there are standards by which the doings of government
may properly be judged.

An open society such as ours is also suspicious of prudence. For
one thing, prudence looks to something other than the sincerity
and frankness of which so much is made among us. Prudence can

almost be seen as deviousness, if not as tyranny, by the democrat.
In any event, prudence takes it for granted that not all men are
equal in certain critical respects and that very few should be at
liberty to do whatever they please. Thus, whereas a tyranny denies
there are any standards by which government might properly be
judged by the governed, an open society is suspicious of any standards by which government might impose its will on the governed.
And especially does this seem to be so when a people make as much
as we Americans do of both liberty and equality.

For our immediate purposes, the often-noticed tension between
liberty and equality can be disregarded. Indeed, it can be said, the
problems of the open society – the critical problems – develop from
the combined abuses (or, at least, effects) of liberty and equality. Of
course, there have always been distinctions drawn between liberty
and license, distinctions which bear upon any consideration of the
open society as well. Similarly, there have always been concerns
about who should be regarded as equals, lest (for example) the
same things be given to unequals.

Have not special twists to these problems developed in the open
society of modernity? Take, for example, the First Amendment
guarantee of "freedom of speech [and] of the press." This guarantee
was once thought to be concerned primarily with political
discourse – discourse carried on in order that a people might be able
truly to govern itself. But, as we now know from the conventional
casebooks in constitutional law, the generally used category here is
no longer "freedom of speech [and] of the press"; rather, it is
"freedom of expression," something which is much more self-
centered and individualistic in its orientation. Thus, the primary
aim of the First Amendment can now be said to be self-realization
or self-fulfillment, not self-government.

For the purpose of self-realization, it is said, the society should be
neutral, certainly with respect to the differences of opinion which
may divide citizens. The liberty of which so much is made is that of
persons, not the liberty of the community itself; and so liberty
means that one should be allowed to do pretty much as one pleases.
But even "allowed" is apt to be considered too intrusive or patroniz-
ing a term, suggesting that the community is deliberately permitting this thing or that. Rather, interferences with persons should
be "minimal": the community should be in principle almost completely oblivious to what is being done. This is what the passion for

liberty can lead to.

The passion for equality, on the other hand, can lead to each believing that his desires are as good as those of the next man. Does not the privacy we make so much of follow from the liberty of enjoying oneself which is exercised by equals? It is in the realm of the private that the "maximum" of personal liberty may be seen among equals. The apolitical (if not anti-political) character of all this – and hence of the open society – should be pointed out: we are, as much as possible, simply to be left alone.

Even if it should be assumed that each man can determine what is his own and that each can be the sort of person he wants to be, it is evident that we cannot, on our own, choose to have the kinds of neighbors and fellow citizens we want or need – unless we are to require the community to do, on our behalf, more in shaping others than it is permitted to do in shaping us. Thus, the liberty we so prize – and prize so much that we wonder whether society should be authoritative in any significant way – may be secured at the expense of equality. That is, others are not to have the kind, or extent, of liberty that *we* have (or rather, that *I* have). If, on the other hand, we do permit others (because all are equal) to have the virtually unbridled liberty we want, then the liberty of all is substantially diminished, since the most important things that affect our lives (what others around us are like and how they conduct themselves) are placed, in principle, beyond our control.

It appears easy to endorse openness for its own sake: it does hold out the considerable attraction of self-gratification. But self-gratification can be at the expense of the community, for, as is said in Plato's *Laws*, "the common binds cities together, while the private tears them apart."[1] "Community," it has been suggested, derives from two Latin words which, when joined, mean "ready to be of service together." Or, as Aristotle put it, men naturally come together for life and stay together for the good life.

"Society," on the other hand, seems to presuppose the *deliberate* establishment of an association, as if men exist (and reason) independent of such coming together. Does not "society" connote something which is more open than is "city" or "country" or "community"? Does not "society" suggest an association that is somehow naturally independent of, or separable from, political life? Is this the form of association that the cult of individuality prefers? Is it that association in which individuality is most potent? In any event, it is society we make so much of, not community. (A community is more likely to be a *commanding* association.) A society, it seems, can much more easily be thought of as open, or set-aside-able, than can a community.

"Openness" suggests that we can be "ourselves," that we are to be unobstructed, that we can be as frank and uninhibited as we please. Of course, all this presupposes that we are or can be "autonomous" beings independent of authoritative guidance from without. It presupposes that there is something intrinsic or natural to us which will somehow or other assert itself; circumstances and training do not matter much. And yet the language in which our desires and self are expressed, if not the very words in which they come to be developed for and known to us, is provided by some community.

However this may be, "openness" suggests that there are no limits, no standards. Is the critical movement, moreover, that of avoidance – with an emphasis upon the absence of confinement or of restraint? Horizons are unbounded. People do speak of "the basic values of an open society." But if openness is taken seriously, there may be nothing basic (that is, enduring or fixed) by which one's bearings should be taken. For would it not be argued that the open society even permits some to restrict themselves severely by completely subjecting themselves to the control of others (if that is how they happen to get their "kicks")?

Modern technology allows, even if it does not encourage, a considerable privatization of associations, of ways of life, and of entertainment. Thus, we do not know (and cannot control) what choices others will make from among the many available to them. Rather, we effectively close ourselves off from each other in the pursuit of our immediate pleasures as we move about anonymously (either among selector switches or along expressways or in large cities). But, in another sense, the open society (backed up by technology) moves us toward radical communism, in that it makes us all share everything: even the most intimate details become subjects for public gossip. Does this make us all feel united, though only on the lowest possible level? Certainly, it is assumed that everything can be exposed to view and, in that sense, shared.

To say that we are all left equally free to choose our own way of life (or, as we now say, "life-style" – thereby tacitly acknowledging the superficiality of our ways of life?) means, in effect, that pleasure is to be (for most people) their guide. But can pleasure be prudently relied upon to guide a free people? Of course, those who have been properly trained, and who have had various imperfections kept out of or purged from their souls, can safely take pleasure for their guide. Pleasure, yes, it can then be said, but the pleasures of the best men; this means that people should be trained to enjoy the best. But such constraint seems antithetical to the open society.

Yet it can also be said, as by Justice Brandeis in his *Whitney* opinion, "Those who won our independence believed that the final end of the State was to make men free to develop their faculties. . . ."[2] And it has been noticed, as in the *Federalist Papers*, "There is in every breast a sensibility to marks of honor, of favor, of esteem, and of confidence, which, apart from all considerations of interest, is some pledge for grateful and benevolent returns."[3] To speak thus of developing faculties and of being guided by honor does suggest that the liberated, the equal, and the personal should give way to the elevated, to the very best of which men are capable when properly prepared. But this is, wherever the open society "asserts" itself, an old-fashioned, if not simply outmoded approach to human relations. This is not to say that the old-fashioned approach does not still have considerable force – after all, nature may be on its side – but it *is* regarded with skepticism among the more fashionable intellectuals of our day. What, then, does the open society "mandate"? Each may go his own way; he is free to do so; he has nothing really better to do than to pursue his own desires; and since equality as well as liberty is made much of, his desires are as good as anyone else's.

Thus, our cherished openness is two-fold: there is nothing outside to stop one; and one is, within, open to everything. The open society results, then, when one's desires (which are "in principle" equal to everyone else's) are given full liberty to be satisfied as each happens to please. It can even extend to permitting men to decide for themselves where they are to live and when life is to begin and to end (as seen by the considerable sympathy shown in the open society for both abortion and suicide).

The open society is, or easily deteriorates into, the shameless society: things are said or not said – done or not done – which would be said and done otherwise wherever a sense of honor or of decorum prevailed. This may be seen in how lawyers, including quite prestigious lawyers, and their clients conduct themselves; it may be seen in how academic faculties (and their administrators) conduct themselves. Thus, top-notch lawyers can be used as shysters would have been in another day; and, thus, faculties can become unduly concerned about their personal well-being and (as in the 1960s) about threats from rebellious students. Few seem to be saying about certain self-protective measures (and this applies as well to matters of national defense), "We do not want this kind of thing done 'on our behalf.' "

The prudent man asks, "Does liberty *have* to be carried so far that we are liberated from moral restraints and from the constraints of honor?" Are these among the inevitable risks of liberty? Perhaps all this is related to, if it is not a natural product of, the remarkable autonomy permitted each of us by private property.

One may go even further: not only is there in the open society much that is shameless about what individuals do, and do openly, in pursuit of gratification (including the gratification of avoidance of a just punishment), but there also is much around us that, in the very fact of its presence or availability, is shameful for us all. That is, we live in a community in which such things *are*, and there is nothing we do about them (or, as we now believe, there is nothing we know of that we can *properly* do about them). Certainly, those who do many of these things feel a certain immunity. And, as has long been known, an absence of fear engenders shamelessness. Of course, there is also something shameful in having to legislate against certain low things: such efforts do admit that something has gone wrong in the community. It is even more shameful, however, when there is little that can be said or done that has an effect on others.

What, one may ask, does shame mean? It is, we have been told, a kind of fear of dishonor.[4] It depends on the opinion of others; and would it not be best *not* to have to rely on such opinions? But for many people that is not feasible, since without community guidance they would be left at the mercy of transitory desires. Besides, should not a decent man be reluctant to do anything that his community clearly disapproves of? We do, however, look up to individualists; we can even insist that it is not a moral question whether one offends the sensibilities of one's neighbors. Still, may not such offenses display a lack of consideration? One should be aware of the limitations of others and not inflict needless pain upon them, merely for one's own gratification. In addition, is there not something ugly in the appearance of extreme selfishness – and something demeaning when that appearance is displayed (if not even justified) before us?

Lawyers, I have indicated, should be saying "No" to clients and would-be clients on many more occasions than they do. (Legislators should be doing the same with constituents. Nor, of course, should academicians simply cater to their students.) Instead, we are accustomed to seeing lawyers vigorously advance their clients' cases as if individual desires and personal interests were all that mattered. (This is related to the notion that freedom of speech and of the press means primarily the right to express oneself as one wishes.) There is much around us, even among the "better" law firms, which suggests that there is indeed "a high correlation between superficial happiness and skullduggery."[5] And so, in the law, we have the problem of the "hired gun," who is available for money. This teaches people what "the brightest and the best" are all too often moved by. If even such lawyers cannot say, "Let those who want or need shysters go to shysters," what are the rest of us (lawyers, politicians and academicians alike) to do?

Let us consider an illustration. (The first half of this article has been devoted more to "theoretical" matters. The second half will be devoted more to "practical" matters, with suggestions about the implications of various routine features of our everyday life.) The police of Bloomingdale, Illinois received an anonymous handwritten letter on May 3, 1978, which read as follows:

> This letter is to inform you that you have a couple in your town who strictly make their living on selling drugs. They are Sue and Lance Gates, they live on Greenway, off Bloomingdale Rd. in the condominiums. Most of their buys are done in Florida. Sue his wife drives their car to Florida, where she leaves it to be loaded up with drugs, then Lance flys [sic] down and drives it back. Sue flys [sic] back after she drops the car off in Florida. May 3 she is driving down there again and Lance will be flying down in a few days to drive it back. At the time Lance drives the car back he has the trunk loaded with over $100,000 in drugs. Presently they have over $100,000 worth of drugs in their basement.
>
> They brag about the fact they never have to work, and make their entire living on pushers.
>
> I guarantee if you watch them carefully you will make a big catch. They are friends with some big drug dealers, who visit their house often.[6]

The letter was referred by the Chief of Police to a detective on his force who decided to pursue the tip. Enough inquiries were made by the police to permit them to be able to anticipate the Gates's return home from a Florida trip. In the meantime, a search warrant for their residence and their automobile had been secured by the police. When the couple returned home on May 7, they were stopped before they entered the house, and their car was searched. Three hundred fifty pounds of marijuana were found in the trunk.

The case raised various technical legal questions, some with good reason. Should the magistrate have issued the search warrant? I gather from my own inquiries that experienced judges who were aware of the then-prevailing law would usually have said "No." Should the police have done more investigating, including extended surveillance of the suspects, before they applied for a search warrant? Perhaps. Their informant *had* assured them that "if you watch them carefully you will make a big catch."

But I am not concerned on this occasion with the technicalities of the law, nor even with the exclusionary rule (for which there may be, in our circumstances, plausible grounds and even some need). Rather, what I am now concerned with, as symptomatic of a certain shamelessness which goes deep, is that both the defendants (apprehended by police who were not acting in any obviously despicable manner) and the defendants' supporters (including their conscientious lawyers) should plead as the defendants did when "caught with the goods." This was an open-and-shut case, with no obvious misconduct on the part of the police. There seems to be no doubt that the defendants in this case had been, for some time, shamelessly exploiting their fellow citizens (and hugely enjoying the privileges of the community). Is there not a curious effrontery to their insistence, in these circumstances, that the community should play by the most technical rules of the game when they themselves had deliberately and repeatedly flouted much more substantial rules of the community? The willingness of people thus compromised to insist on their "rights" seems to reflect a "commitment" among us to "individuality," which in turn may go back to an emphasis on self-preservation as fundamental. Anything goes, we have been told, as one tries to save oneself.

Still, it will be said, one can expect such shamelessness when one deals with the kind of people who deliberately run afoul of the law as did these drug dealers. Such people are on the fringes of society and otherwise marginal. There may be something to this kind of comment. Still, should not even those on the fringes (once their misconduct has been exposed to public view) be more susceptible to the force of public opinion than has become fashionable?

But then, public opinion has lost its self-confidence. A symptom of this may be seen not only in the response to, but in the timing if not the very existence of, a recent television show. Thus, it is reported:

> One in every three of us is tuning in on TV's latest mini-series, ABC's *The Thorn Birds* – even though there are complaints about its airing during a week of religious observances.
>
> The steamy sex-and-religion drama gained an estimated 80 million viewers across the USA Sunday – higher than the opener of ABC's successful *Winds of War* in February.

The timing of this show is noticed in this report:

> Not everyone is enjoying it: Roman Catholics protest its broadcast during Holy Week. Jewish viewers are complaining the second and third part fall on Passover nights, when families busy with Seder observances won't be able to watch.[7]

Should not such blatant disregard for, if not distortion of, religious sensibilities remind us of the dubious status of organized religion for most advocates today of the open society?

But perhaps this sort of thing, too, can be considered on the fringes – and hence not representative. Since I rarely see television, perhaps the most dramatic indication I personally have had recently of what has been going on among us came when I happened to have a few hours to spare in a town near where I grew up in southern Illinois.

A popular movie happened to be showing in the theatre. We were a full house. The movie did have good things about it (including useful indications, however exaggerated, of the proper preparations for doing one's duty as a flying officer.) But there were also "steamy" sex scenes (to use the language applied to *The Thorn Birds* mini-series) which left little to the imagination. The audience sharing all this looked quite respectable and included high school youngsters. I could not help but observe that all this had been legitimated for everyone to see in the very town where I had dated a very nice girl four decades before. And I could not help but wonder whether her teenage children or grandchildren might be in such an audience somewhere. One can be saddened upon so wondering.

It should go without saying that I do not believe I have any objection to healthy sensuality (whatever reservations I may have about the "sexual revolution" of our time and about the uninformed opinions that have made it possible). I am not necessarily objecting to what the rather acrobatic young couple on the movie screen were *doing*, but rather *where* they were doing it (that is, in front of us). Indeed, this kind of sharing (that is, by the loving couple on the screen with others) is likely, in time, to make genuine sharing difficult, if not impossible, for "real people." Critical, then, to the open – or rather, *opened up* and dismantled – society may be not only the subversion of community but also the perversion, if not paralysis, of genuine intimacy.

The southern Illinois town in which I saw my enlightening movie must still have the same population it had in my time there. Or, rather, its numbers are the same – some ten thousand souls – but not the character of its people. The very fact that that movie could be so casually shown to a full house, with no one getting up to leave, all this – which is repeated innumerable times all over the country (for it *is* a popular movie, with even an Academy Award now to its credit) – informs, or at least reminds us that profound changes have taken place in this country since the Second World War. That period aroused great passions, brought about profound dislocations, and got us accustomed to massive institutional and technological changes which had been prepared for by the Great Depression.

I turn now to a brief consideration of how this dramatic change of character (or, at least, of conduct) of the American people has come about. I refer not to decisive underlying opinions about equality, community, and liberty, or about the supposed subjectivity of moral precepts. I refer rather to social developments (due both to these opinions and to chance) which have helped break down the natural inclination of a sound people to enforce the rules about propriety it has long believed in. Among the social developments relevant here are those associated with the "mass media." I have had occasion, for example, to consider in print the significance of television among us. And this has led me to develop the proposal that broadcast television in this country should be abolished.[8]

I gather that television has become even worse than it was when I studied it a decade ago. Certainly, *I* find it ever worse whenever I encounter it. It is appalling what the bulk of my fellow citizens are being constantly exposed to – and corrupted by. (Particularly significant is how much local communities are being affected by the national networks.) I had been aware, before attending that movie, of what had been happening in the entertainment industry – but I had not recognized that there had already been as deep an effect as there evidently has been. What makes such changes less noticeable than they should be is that so much around us remains the same, such as how church people look and sound: they continue to resemble their counterparts in small towns two generations ago.

The developments I describe can be expected to become even worse as technology "progresses": as cable television and video cassettes become more and more accessible, we can expect more and more bizarre things to become available (as well as, of course, a *few* good things). Each will then be able to order up his own particular "mix" of thrills and other forms of self-gratification; and this will mean, among other things, that we as a community will have even less in common. Be all this as it may, television *is* the source of the new reality: it is the new legitimator. A thing is not real until it is seen on television. But all this, I am afraid, is commonplace – or, at least, should be.

Preceding, accompanying and reinforcing the effects of television are various much more prosaic developments – such as the modernization of our national highway system and the great success of shopping centers in this country. These have helped make possible the radical implementation of "advanced" opinions about the open society among us, a development into which our experiments with television and movies easily fit. Various such innovations have intensified the privatization that property rights tend to promote. Expressways and shopping centers have a combined effect: both tend to be destructive of an attractive downtown life in American towns and cities. Assembly areas are created with easy means to get to them, to which people go primarily for commerce and commercialized entertainment, areas in which they gather for quite limited times according to special interests. The old downtown was a place where the entire community mingled, more or less continuously, in the ordinary course of living and on its own (that is, on the community's) property.

Consider a recent experience I had in a Pennsylvania town in which we found ourselves (having deliberately left the interstate highway to do so). It was late at night; we preferred to stop at a hotel there, so we could walk around town that night and early the next morning. But no downtown hotel was still in business; we had to settle for a characterless motel on the highway. One *could* see in the town center – the predecessor of the shopping center – a massive courthouse and several monuments from great wars. One got thereby a sense of a genuine community, one for which men had fought and died and in which justice had been given the trappings of dignity. In short, one gets the impression, from such places, of communities in which people live and die. Even old-fashioned cemeteries are more vital, more alive, than are many modern shopping centers with their glittery facades.

How have shopping centers come to be? On the basis, usually, of private entrepreneurial decisions about which the community has really had little to say. And because someone believes, with good reason, that he can do better for *himself* by developing a shopping center, the integrity of the community is severely compromised.

The remarkable expansion of our highways can be traced in part to a generation-long concern for military preparedness. An intensification of regard for the self goes along with an emphasis upon self-preservation. Government is permitted, if not encouraged, to go to great lengths to protect our bodies, even while it is kept from attempting to improve our souls. Out of this has come, among other things, the interstate highway system, which has isolated most American towns from the long-distance traveller and has made it easy for inhabitants of towns to range far and wide, out of the range of their neighbors' observation.

It does seem, on the basis of the things I have noticed on this occasion, that the open society (as we know it) is largely one in which commercial relations and commercial calculations (in the broadest sense of "commerce") are critical. That is, an economic, or utilitarian, approach seems to govern, an approach which encourages and equips each individual to look out for his interests as *he* happens to see them. It also makes much of innovations, innovations which there is really no way of predicting or (it would now seem) of controlling. We seem, then, to be unduly subject to chance. This is not an altogether new set of alternatives – between controlling and not controlling where the country will go and what it will be–as may be seen in the Lincoln-Douglas debates. But there is one thing absent from the national debate today, and that is a well-reasoned public argument (by liberal-minded citizens) which insists that moral considerations are very much within the deliberate power and the informed duty of the people of the United States, as self-governing, to take into account and to act upon as prudence dictates in varying circumstances.

To refer thus to prudence is to remind ourselves of the political problems we confront, and of the proper ends of government in the service of which prudence is to be employed. The people need a few among them, at least from time to time, to draw out the implications of what has been happening to them. They also need to be reassured that their almost instinctive regard for the community, in the face of an all-too-prevalent self-centeredness, is indeed sound. Furthermore, they need to have pointed out to them what a sound community looks like and how happy a truly healthy life should be.

In addition, the people need to be reminded of their prerogatives and their powers. A few summers ago, I had a conversation with an influential Midwestern banker who was concerned about the shopping center which was about to be developed outside his hometown, which still had a vital downtown. The most striking thing about this conversation was the apparent helplessness of this man: he was not prepared to try to do anything (for example, promulgate county zoning laws) which would discourage such a shopping center. What was critical to his unwillingness to try something was not an inability to think of remedies, but rather his obvious lack of conviction: he simply did not believe he had the "right" to keep others from spending their money as they wished (so long as they did not resort to violence or fraud). Thus, we again see the civic paralysis induced by the lack of self-confidence on the part of the community.

I do not mean to suggest by all this that the institution of private property has not been vital among us: in fact, it has been essential to the considerable freedom we cherish and depend upon. The question remains, however: What *is* the master art? Should not uses of private property be subordinated, ultimately, to reasoned political concerns for the common good? But are not Americans generally trapped, as was the Midwestern banker, by doctrines which, however useful they may be for many purposes, can be subversive of the proper ends of the community?

These doctrines, which I have several times touched upon here in my exploration of the open society, are nicely suggested by the mottoes on the Government Department building I happened upon recently at Lafayette College in Easton, Pennsylvania. The "Hall of Civil Rights," finished in 1929, prominently displays these mottoes: "Every man is the architect of his own fortune"; "Every man is free to do what he will, provided he infringes not the equal freedom of any other man"; and, on the front, "Is it not lawful for me to do what I will with my own?" Nicely evident in these mottoes is the assumption that men do have as their own, independent of the community, such things as property.

Can anything be done about the shortcomings of the open society? It should go without saying that the unexamined opinions upon which much of modern development depends should be examined, including what we mean by "property." And it would certainly help if a sense of honor were revived among us, at least to the extent necessary for a restoration of a susceptibility to shame. Legislation, in its broadest sense, should be considered to mold the opinions that shape us and to regulate the activities that shape us and influence our opinions. Thus, both fundamental questions and prosaic conduct should be addressed.

It should be evident that in any proper program of re-education, or revitalization, of the American people as sovereign public, the First Amendment should be given its rightful place.[9] Not only does it *not* keep us from regulating (even to the extent of eliminating) television and obscenity *as we deliberately choose*, and not only does it *not* keep us from implementing sound programs in moral training, but it is vital to the efforts of the people and their leaders to examine thoroughly where we are and where we should go. (Freedom of speech and of the press means that whatever is done about such things as commerce, television, moral training, obscenity, and search warrants can be thoroughly examined and amended from time to time by the sovereign community.)

That the freedom of speech and of the press protected by the First Amendment – a freedom primarily that of citizens discussing public measures and public men – may also be abused from time to time goes without saying. But there does not seem to be, except in the most acute emergency, any constitutional way (by the use of direct government action) to suppress some political discourse without endangering the effectiveness of all political discourse.

To speak thus of the First Amendment is to reassert the prerogatives of the community, a community which is equipped and entitled to judge and to act. It is also to question the claims and ultimate tendencies of the open society, hedonistic tendencies which culminate in an anarchy which is likely to stimulate an unhealthy concern for self-preservation. This means, in effect, that the thoughtless open society is particularly open to tyranny.

I do not believe that the Founding Fathers ever spoke as we do of the open society. If they did it was perhaps only incidentally, and then as a result of the influence of the Enlightenment (which was, in some curious ways, apolitical in its assumptions and projects). What they did clearly speak of, and of which "open society" may be a perversion, is "candid world"–which, in the Declaration of Independence, is addressed and appealed to:

> The History of the present King of Great-Britain is a History of repeated Injuries and Usurpations, all having in direct Object the Establishment of an absolute Tyranny over these States. To prove this, let Facts be submitted to a candid World.

"Candid world" means, it seems, a world open to "the facts"–that is, to experience and argument. This assumes, among other things, that there are standards that sensible communities around the world can be expected to respect, standards that permit men to recognize usurpations and tyranny for what they are. The authors of the Declaration of Independence then go on to set forth, at the very heart of that document, a catalogue of abuses and grievances for "a candid World" to consider.

Thus, it was not enough for eighteenth-century Americans to insist upon their equality or to assert their liberty. They believed themselves obliged to show that they were entitled, in their circumstances, to say and to do things that a prudent community is entitled to do and to say, in the expectation that other prudent men all over the world would recognize and endorse the merits of their arguments. Such reasoned rhetoric is a far cry from the indulgence in mere self-expression that sometimes seems the hallmark of open societies deaf to the dictates of that prudence which serves both the common good and human perfection.

Notes

* Extensive notes for this essay may be found in the version published in *The Willamette Law Review* (Fall 1984).

¹ Plato, *Laws* 875a.

² *Whitney* v. *California*, 274 U.S. 357, 375 (1927) (concurring opinion). James Wilson observed in the Constitutional Convention of 1787, "[I cannot] agree that [the protection of] property [is] the sole or the primary object of government and society. The cultivation and improvement of the human mind [is] the most noble object." See Anastaplo, *Human Being and Citizen: Essays on Virtue, Freedom and the Common Good* (Chicago: Swallow Press, 1975), 120.

³ *Federalist* no. 57.

⁴ See Aristotle, *Nicomachean Ethics*, bk. IV, chap. 9. See my essay, "Aristotle on Law and Morality," appended to a book review in *The Windsor Yearbook of Access to Justice*, vol. 3 (1983).

⁵ Harris Wofford, Jr., ed., *Embers of the World: Conversations with Scott Buchanan* (Santa Barbara, Calif.: Center for the Study of Democratic Institutions, 1970), 203. See, on Abraham Lincoln as a principled yet successful lawyer, Anastaplo, "Mr. Justice Black, His Generous Common Sense and The Bar Admission Cases," *Southwestern University Law Review* 9 (1977) : 977, 1033-1034. See also, "Law Professor is Still Denied License to Practice," *The New York Times*, 11 Sept. 1983, p. 30; *National Law Journal*, 22 Aug. 1983, p. 8, 12 Sept. 1983, p. 12, 14 Nov. 1983, p. 19. See, as well, Anastaplo, "Mr. Crosskey, the American Constitution, and the Natures of Things," *Loyola University of Chicago Law Journal* 15 (1983), notes 24 and 25; Anastaplo, *The Artist as Thinker: From Shakespeare to Joyce* (Chicago: Swallow Press/Ohio University Press, 1983), chap. 1.

⁶ Illinois v. Gates, 76 L. Ed. 2d 527, 540 (1983).

⁷ *USA Today*, 19 March 1983, p. 1.

⁸ See Anastaplo, "Self-Government and the Mass Media: A Practical Man's Guide," in Harry M. Clor, ed., *The Mass Media and Modern Democracy* (Chicago: Rand McNally, 1974).

⁹ See, on freedom of speech and the First Amendment, Anastaplo, "Censorship," *Encyclopedia Britannica*, 15th ed.; *The Constitutionalist: Notes on the First Amendment* (Dallas: Southern Methodist University Press, 1971). It should be evident from this article that acceptable cures for the ills of the open society are not likely to be found in various tyrannical (that is, closed) societies of our time.

What Price an Open Society?

Henry Veatch

Let me begin by first indicating what I hope one would not take the notion of "the open society" to be, and then go on to suggest what I hope one might take it to be. For is it not at once conceivable, and yet unfortunate, that people consider the openness of an open society to be an openness to a kind of organic growth and development – i.e., to a specifically societal evolution and eventual flourishing of the social whole itself? Yet, is a society the kind of being or entity that can, either in a literal or an analogous sense, be open to any proper kind of biological growth, development or maturity? Alas, being but a would-be Aristotelian in philosophy, I can only react to this by noting that surely any Aristotelian would feel constrained to say that anything like a polis, or a society, or a state, is quite incapable of anything like a natural growth or development, since a society is not a "substance." Thus, in anything like a plant or an animal, for example, one can certainly say that the functioning and well-being of the parts of the organism are to be completely subordinated to the flourishing and well-functioning of the whole. But can one say this of a state or society or human community?

Why, then, might I not simply call the openness to development that is characteristic of a biological organism a *holistic openness*, meaning that it is an openness to the eventual flourishing of the organism itself, taken as a whole? But when it comes to a human society or community, anything like a holistic openness, it would seem, is just not relevant or appropriate. Instead, a society's openness needs to be construed, not as an openness to the flourishing of the whole, to which the functioning of the parts would thus need to be subordinated, but rather as an openness to the flourishing and well-being of the individuals who make up that society. Putting it very crudely, I would declare that, unlike biological organisms, in human communities and human societies the whole exists for the sake of the parts, and not the other way around. Or, to put it differently, a human society exists to no other end, and to no other purpose, than to foster and secure the well-being of its individual members. Call this, if you will, an *individualistic openness*, as contrasted to a holistic openness.

Non-human societies – termites, bees, herds, flocks, coveys, etc. – can scarcely be conceived of as being substances in any Aristotelian sense; and yet clearly, in the cases of these non-human societies, the well-being of the members needs to be conceived of as being subordinated to the maintenance and well-being of the group as a whole, or of the entire species considered over time. Let me simply affirm in passing, however, that it just is not proper to consider human societies in this way at all. No, human societies, I will say, are only rightly open if in them the social whole exists solely to promote the well-being of the individual members. In other words, with human societies the proper sort of openness can only be individualistic, not holistic.

And with this there will no doubt be rained down upon me the violent protests of ever so many sophisticated social philosophers who like to think of themselves as being social organicists in some sense or other – Hegelians, Marxists, socio-biologists perhaps; Romantics of the type of Herder, or even historians like the great von Ranke; and yes, even the one-time *Blut-und-Boden* enthusiasts of Hitler's Third Reich. Perhaps, though, the norm for such social organicists might rather be the far more respectable British Hegelians of the latter part of the last century and the beginning of this century – figures like T.H. Green and F.H. Bradley. Bradley's repeated declaration of principle was that "the good is simply the good of the whole." Accordingly, what I am now proposing is that, in that individualistic openness with respect to human societies that I would champion, one would need to stand Bradley's slogan right on its head and proclaim: in human societies it is the whole that exists for the sake of the parts, never the parts for the sake of the whole, at least not as such.

In coming down on the side of an individualistic, rather than of a holistic openness, I certainly to not mean to associate myself with old-fashioned classical liberalism or the new-fashioned libertarianism whose proponents are today the most obvious champions of an individualistic openness. After all, do they not insist that human society exists to no other end or purpose than to further the interests and rights of individual members of society – these conceived as being ultimately the interest and right of each individual simply to live his own life, to follow his own tastes and inclinations, as far as possible, without having to concern himself with dictation or interference from the outside, particularly such as might come from the state, polis, or society as a whole? On the liberal view anything like a governance of the individual by political or social agencies must be reduced to the barest minimum. Or at least, so it would seem to be in some such sense as this that what we have been calling an individualistic openness in society would presumably be construed by present-day liberals and libertarians.

But the implied assumption that one might think had emerged in the course of the preceding remarks is at once unwarranted and not really compelling. This is the assumption that any social order characterized by an individualistic openness cannot be other than a social order of the familiar liberal or libertarian type.[1] However, we must now consider whether a so-called liberal society can ever be viable, much less philosophically well-founded. For what, after all, is the basic principle upon which any open or free society, conceived in the spirit of modern liberalism, might be based? Is not such a principle that of certain basic and inalienable rights of the human individuals who make up the society – rights which in the familiar terminology of the eighteenth century are said to be "natural rights"? Moreover, the sense in which such rights are natural is that the human individual enjoys them in a so-called state of nature, prior to any condition which he may come to have within civil society – for example, rights to such things as life, liberty and property. Such rights, being possessed by individuals simply by virtue of their original human nature, can therefore be claimed as, in principle, inalienable by any subsequent social or political organization: what is ours by nature is something that we cannot rightfully be deprived of by subsequent political or social convention or organization.

For example, consider how Locke chose to formulate the terms of that original charter or title-deed that any human individual supposedly has to a right or freedom to live his own life as he chooses and sees fit:

> To understand political power right, and derive it from its original, we must consider what state all men are naturally in, and that is, *a state of perfect freedom* to order their actions and dispose of their possessions and persons as they think fit. . . .[2]

Moreover, since it may be recalled that Locke considers that, correlated with this "state of perfect freedom," there is also a state of perfect equality, we might complete the above quotation with the one which immediately follows it:

> A *state* also *of equality*, wherein all the power and jurisdiction is reciprocal, no one having more than another; there being nothing more evident, than that creatures of the same species and rank, promiscuously born to all the same advantages of nature, and the use of the same faculties, should also be equal one amongst another without subordination or subjection. . . .[3]

But on what ground is it exactly that Locke would thus seem to claim that any human individual has a right to such freedom and equality? Now would it not appear, at least superficially, that Locke's argument turns out to be either no argument at all, or else a patently fallacious one? For what else would Locke seem to be doing in the passages just cited, if not claiming that in the state of nature, and prior to their being in any state of civil society, all human beings are in fact free and equal?

Suppose we grant Locke this much. Still, from the fact that men *are* thus free by nature – "free to order their actions and dispose of their possessions and persons as they think fit" – does it in any wise follow that men therefore *ought to be* free, or have a *right* to such freedom? Is not such an argument from a *fact* to a *right*, or, as Hume was later to put it, from an "is" to an "ought," simply to commit a fallacy? Yes, what we have here is nothing other than just that is-ought fallacy, which is now become so much the stock in trade of contemporary moral philosophers that they seem to want to invoke it almost at every whipstitch.

And what does this do, if not seriously undermine any case for an individualistic openness, conceived after the fashion of either classical liberalism or latter-day libertarianism? For does not the case for any such liberalism rest upon the basic claim that human individuals have rights – rights that antedate social institutions, and that therefore cannot rightfully be taken away from individuals by any conventions or laws of society? Yet now it would appear that there are no such rights, or at least that the argument for such rights, involving an inference from facts to rights, or from "is" to "ought," turns out to be nothing if not a patent *non sequitur*.

Even if these same rights were capable of being properly proved and established, are they not often seriously in conflict with one another; or, if not in conflict with one another, then at least are they not frequently inconsistent even each with itself? For instance, as for the inconsistency of these rights one with another, the criticism has long been made that the two basic rights which Locke mentions – the right of men to freedom and at the same time to equality – must sooner or later conflict with one another. If you, for instance, in the free exercise of your abilities, come to outstrip me in both property and power, then why may I not complain that my natural equality with you – and hence my right to being equal in status with you – has been seriously jeopardized? Moreover, if the civil community or polis in which you and I both live should, as a consequence of this emergent inequality between you and me, attempt to redress the supposed natural balance between us, would this not have to be done by imposing serious restrictions upon your freedom, in order that my natural equality with you might thereby be restored? And what is this if not a situation in which, of our two basic rights to freedom and to equality, the one must almost inevitably be compromised in favor of the other?

Consider briefly how our supposedly basic natural right to freedom and liberty turns out to be almost inescapably a right that is curiously inconsistent even with itself. Already we have seen how this right to liberty is customarily interpreted to mean that an individual is free to do whatever he wants with whatever is his own – with his life, his liberty and his property, in other words. But no sooner is an individual's right to freedom and liberty of action thus enunciated, than almost immediately the qualification gets added that, of course, an individual can do whatever he wants with himself and his life and property, provided that he not impede or interfere with others in their exercise of their comparable rights.

And yet is there not a patent inconsistency here? One might rightfully say that within the context of liberalism and a liberal society, the individual is given two basic instructions or imperatives: (1) feel free to follow your own inclinations and do as you please; and (2) don't allow this freedom or liberty on your part to interfere with a like freedom and liberty on the part of your fellow citizens or fellow human beings. Surely, though, these two injunctions of the liberal state are scarcely compatible with each other. Blackstone realized as much when he wrote:

> The principal aim of society is to protect individuals in the enjoyment of those absolute rights [and by absolute rights here Blackstone would specify the rights to life, liberty, and property] which were vested in them by the immutable laws of nature, but which could not be preserved in peace, without the mutual assistance and intercourse of social communities. The primary end of human laws is to maintain and regulate these absolute rights of individuals.[4]

Notice that what Blackstone would here seem to be saying quite unequivocally is that an individual's rights – say, my rights to life, liberty, and property – are "absolute." But then, is it not somewhat ironical, not to say puzzling, that no sooner am I thus assured that my rights to these things are absolute, than my liberal tutor, be it a Blackstone in the eighteenth century or someone like Rawls today, will turn right around and tell me that my right to liberty is really not absolute after all? Thus to quote Rawls, for example, my right to liberty, so far from being absolute, is only a right to "the most extensive basic liberty compatible with a similar liberty for others." But with that bland announcement, has not a liberal like Rawls bitten a truly enormous chunk right out of that otherwise tasty morsel of liberty that had been held out to me in the first place? So large a chunk, in fact, that one wonders if there is much of a morsel of liberty left. Talk about the right hand not knowing what the left hand is doing; maybe it is rather a case of the right hand knowing very well what the left hand is doing, the whole show being but a conjuring trick whereby the liberal takes back with one hand the liberty or freedom that he has just given with the other.

Oh, but you will say, I am only being petulant, not to say sophistic, about this. And indeed, upon reflection, do I not have to acknowledge that I can scarcely claim a freedom or a liberty for myself without recognizing that others are just as entitled to such a freedom or liberty as I am, and that therefore the exercise of my own liberty has got to be made compatible with the exercise of a like liberty on the part of others? Granted. And yet is not the obvious answer to this simply to challenge the argument in its entirety?

Thus just where, I might ask, do these so-called "others" that I am supposed to have a regard for come from, and how did they get into the picture in the first place? For what was the nature and character of that original right to liberty that the liberal said he was extending to me at the outset? Call it, if you will, a sort of *Ur*-right to liberty that the liberal presumably assured me was mine in the state of nature and outside of society. Already we have seen that such a right meant simply the right of the individual to do his own thing, to lead his own life, to engage in his own pursuit of happiness – whatever that individual's tastes and preferences might be, and regardless of what others might think of such preferences, whether they might like them or not or approve of them or not. In other words, if this be the way that the basic right to liberty in the liberal program is originally conceived and understood, then there is no way in which, subsequently and with any consistency, the liberal could then turn around and say that my right to live my own life regardless of others is at the same time a right that must be qualified and restricted out of regard for these others.

Nor will it do any good for someone to try to invoke the so-called Principle of Universalizability at this point.[5] Not that there is anything wrong with the principle as such: if anyone may claim a right to something simply on the basis of his being human, then it would certainly seem that any other human being ought to be able to claim a similar right, and for a like reason. But the question is: is such a principle as that of Universalizability applicable in this instance? After all, if the right I claim initially turns out to be incompatible with others' possessing and exercising the same right, then there is no way in which it could ever be universalized. Specifically, if my initial right to liberty be conceived and defined in such a way as to preclude any and all interference with that liberty from the outside, then how could that right possibly be universalized in such a way as to render just such outside interference and restriction not merely possible, but practically inescapable? Surely, this is getting close to a veritable *contradictio in adjecto*.

Nor is this the most serious objection to this argument. For the argument is that if, by virtue of my being a human being, I can claim a right to do as I wish and live as I please, then by the Principle of Universalizability any and every other human being may be said to have a similar and equal right. But suppose that one grants this principle to be quite unexceptionable. Still, the prior question is whether it has been established that any human being does have a right to live as he pleases and to do with his own whatever he wishes. Already we have seen how Locke's claim that individuals have a right to freedom and equality – or Blackstone's claim that individuals have rights of life, liberty, and property – would not appear to have been adequately supported or justified. On the contrary, the mere supposition that human beings *are* free, or *are* equal by nature, provides no ground whatever for the inference that therefore human beings have a *right* to such freedom and equality. For this would be tantamount to an inference from "is" to "ought." And if the fact that human beings are free and equal by nature does not suffice to establish that they have a right to such freedom and equality, then what other grounds have been adduced, or can be adduced, in support of the supposed natural rights of individuals?

Accordingly, if individuals cannot be shown to have any rights in the first place, the invocation of the Principle of Universalizability will be to no effect whatever. True, if any one man has such rights, then all do – and this by that principle. However, if the evidence is lacking that even any one has such rights by nature, then one might almost say that the principle works to the opposite effect: it not being able to be shown that anyone has rights, it presumably follows that none do!

Now where do we stand? Alas, we don't seem to stand on any firm ground as regards either liberalism or libertarianism, or even as regards supposedly basic individual human rights. But if there is, then, no real ground for individual rights, how can we possibly support the idea of "the open society" – at least, not if it is to be conceived in terms of what we have called an individualistic, as contrasted with a holistic, type of openness. Are we left with no other choice than to subscribe to a distinctively holistic type of openness as our only viable alternative? After all, is it not just such a holistic option that, in one form or another, tends to be the option of ever so many present-day conservatives the minute they become disenchanted with the prospects for a liberal state or society?

But no, I can't see myself as either inclined or necessitated to go the way of this conservative or holistic option. Instead, why isn't it possible to stick with our earlier option of an individualistic type of openness, holding that any true openness of a society should be nothing if not an openness to the free development of the individuals within the society? Yet at the same time, might it not be possible that an individualistic openness could be understood in such a way as to obviate its mere collapse into the liberalism of the liberal state? Yes, but how is such a thing to be brought off?

As an initial step toward meeting this challenge, let me point out that while, of course, it can be only the happiness and well-being of the individual citizens that is the end of any truly open society, there are nevertheless quite different ways of conceiving this same happiness and well-being. Put yourself in the position of an individual within an open society which is presumably devoted to promoting the well-being of those within it: just how would you construe that happy condition for yourself that presumably you, and the open society in which you were living, were trying to bring about? What is it, in other words, that you want for yourself as an individual? What do you take the good life to be?

Would you not need to recognize two quite different types of answers to such questions? On the one hand, would it not be plausible to suppose that the good life would be simply doing what you want, following your own interests, inclinations, and preferences? At the same time, on the other hand, might there perhaps be a more objective standard for determining what is best for you, or what a truly good life for a human being should consist in? Thus it is not entirely inconceivable that a particular individual might think certain things would surely make you happy, only to find out that, once you had attained such things, they did not make you happy at all, but only left you that much the more miserable because of your being thus disappointed? As an even more extreme possibility, it is by no means inconceivable that a given individual might be so blind to the realities of his own situation that he might think himself to be quite happy and well off, whereas to any perceptive outside observer the poor devil was living in nothing less that a fool's paradise.

In fact, Jane Austen very neatly depicts a character just such as this in her account of one Sir Walter Elliott in the novel

Persuasion:

> Sir Walter Elliott of Kellynch Hall, in Somersetshire, was a man who, for his own amusement, never took up any book but the Baronetage; there he found occupation for an idle hour and consolation in a distressed one. . . .
> Vanity was the beginning and end of Sir Walter Elliott's character: vanity of person and of situation. He had been remarkably handsome in his youth, and at fifty-four was still a very fine man. Few women could think more of their personal appearance than he did, nor could the valet of any new made lord be more delighted with the place he held in society. He considered the blessings of beauty as inferior only to the blessing of a baronetcy; and the Sir Walter Elliott who united these gifts, was the constant object of his warmest respect and devotion.[6]

Certainly, no one could have been more satisfied and contented with himself and his lot than Sir Walter. In his own eyes he was a happy man. And yet quite patently, the man was nothing but a pompous ass. And so there would surely seem to be good reason for any of us, when we take thought for our own happiness and well-being, at least to stop and consider whether as individuals we need rely simply on our own immediate preferences and inclinations, or whether there might rather be more objective standards of an individual's well-being that perhaps could and should be employed in such cases.

In any case, this ambiguity – or, if you will, this duality – of interpretations as to what our personal happiness or well-being really is, and how such a thing may best be determined, is most tellingly brought out in Plato's dialogue, the *Euthyphro*. In fact, I have been wont to coin the term "the *Euthyphro* test," as if this might be a kind of touchstone for determining, in any given individual's case, what the two alternative ways are in which one might try to determine just what it is that one's own happiness and well-being might amount to and consist in. For recall how, in the dialogue, Socrates asks the question, Are we to say that things are good, because they are beloved of the gods; or are they beloved of the gods because they are good?

Translated into our present context, the import of this Socratic question or test would come down to something like this: when we talk about what men's ends or goals are, or what the human good or human well-being or human happiness must needs consist in, do we mean to imply that certain things are good for men merely because they happen to like them, or desire them, or "go for" them; or is it rather that certain things are good for men because it is just such things that men ought to desire, or like, or seek after, whether they actually do or not?

Granted that there are these two different sorts of ways or standards that men tend to apply for determining what it is that their happiness and well-being as individuals – yes, their very ends and purposes in life – ought to consist in, might this perhaps be of some import for the defensibility of an individualistic openness in a given society, whether the happiness and the well-being of the individuals were to be judged on the more subjective, or the more objective, model under the *Euthyphro* test? Even more specifically, is it possible that the very failings of a liberal or libertarian type of society might perhaps be traceable to the fact that, in the context of such liberalism, there just aren't any objective standards at all for individual conduct, aims, and ends in life? Instead, in a liberal society, the individual is never obligated to observe any objective standards regarding the human good, or regarding what his own aims and ends in life ought to be. On the contrary, the principle always is that a person is free to do whatever he wants, provided always that he not interfere with others in their doing what they want – a proviso which we have already noted seems incapable of any adequate philosophical justification.

Moreover, was it not just this that proved to be the ineradicable weakness of any liberal or libertarian conception of openness in a society? For there would seem to be no way in which any properly moral justification or moral worth could ever be found in individuals' simply doing as they pleased, following their own inclinations, or doing what they were already impelled to do anyway. In other words, it was doubtless because it proved to be impossible ever to show that it was in any sense morally right that an individual should simply do whatever he liked, that it therefore should have proved no less impossible to show that individuals thus had any sort of moral or natural right to do whatever they wanted to do.

In contrast, suppose that it is the other model that was suggested under the *Euthyphro* test that is to be operative in determining what an individual's aims and objectives should be within the context of an open society. This is the model according to which those things an individual takes to be good, or his true ends in life, are not ends or goods merely because the individual takes them to be so, and thus tends to desire them and to pursue them; rather, it is the other way around: it is because the individual recognizes that he has certain natural ends, and that his life is ordered to a certain natural perfection and fulfillment, that he thus comes to desire such things and to pursue them as being his true end or his true good. Given this alternative framework for an understanding of individualism, it could then be that in a society devoted to an individualistic openness, the individual would not necessarily have to be thought of as being left free to do whatever he might please; rather, his freedom would be of a sort that would enable him to choose his own course of action in accordance with what his reason or intelligence might tell him his true ends were, and what his proper good or perfection as a human individual should be. Why, in other words, might this not offer a prospect for a *morally principled* individualism, as contrasted with an individualism based on mere whims, likings, and personal idiosyncrasies?

Before we can address ourselves directly to the question of whether a human individualism, conceived in the one way under the *Euthyphro* test, might better make an individualistic openness in society a more tenable and viable political option than would an individualism conceived under the other model, we should first consider the respective philosophical contexts into which these two sorts of individualisms can best be fitted, and from which they can best be understood. Already, we have seen something of what the proper philosophical setting might be for a liberal or libertarian individualism. For is it not from out of a background of something like a state of nature that such an individualism has so often been attempted to be understood? At least, such was Hobbes's view of the matter, as well as Locke's; and so it also seems to be the viewpoint of thinkers like Rawls and Nozick in our own day. However, since it is especially Hobbes who had the more original insights into a philosophical setting for liberalism and the liberal society, let us look to him.

Hobbes was writing at a time when the great scientific revolution of the seventeenth century had just burst upon the consciousness of thinkers in Western Europe. With his unerring perspicacity, Descartes had already seen that the new physical universe could not be other than a radically amoral or non-moral universe. Not only were there no final causes in the universe of the new physics; there weren't any values, either, or any standards of right or wrong. In fact, to take but a crude example, consider a naively phrased law of nature to the effect that water seeks its own level. And now suppose we ask if it is right or wrong that water should seek its own level; or, when water does attain to its own level, we cheer and say, "Bravo! Water, you have really brought it off this time"; or, on the contrary, should it happen that the water be impeded in reaching its own level, we say, "Too bad!" or "Naughty, naughty, Water, you should have done better than that." Quite patently, all these questions and reactions are not just out of place; they are ridiculous on their face, in the context of modern physical science and physical nature.

When Hobbes imagines human individuals as being in a state of nature, it is a nature where absolutely no moral guidelines or standards of value are to be found. Instead, it being a state of nature and not of society, human beings are literally bound by no laws either moral or civil, but only by physical laws. Accordingly, there being no moral laws, nothing that a person does in the state of nature is either right or wrong, good or bad. And accordingly, in this sense any individual in the state of nature may be said to be "free" to do whatever he likes – which is to say that he is free from any moral or political restraints, subject only to the operation of purely physical forces and powers. Hence, there is nothing *wrong* with whatever any individual happens to do in such a state of nature, it being *all right* for him to do whatever he pleases, there being no law (moral or civil) against it. Yet note that to say it is "all right" for an individual in the state of nature to do whatever he pleases, or that there is nothing "wrong" in his so doing, is still a far cry from saying that it is morally right for the individual thus to act merely on his own impulses and inclinations. The mere absence of moral prohibitions against certain courses of action certainly does not mean that such actions are morally right in any positive moral sense. Quite the contrary: to infer as much would make one guilty of a patent *non sequitur*. In other words, in a Hobbesian state of nature, it is neither right nor wrong that individuals should act as they do. Instead, whatever they do is completely amoral, or morally neutral.

Moreover, is it not clear from this brief sketch that it is precisely

a Hobbesian freedom of this sort that supposedly provides the basis
for the sort of freedom that is championed in a liberal society, on
the ground that it is man's freedom by right of nature? But is it not
equally clear that such a freedom becomes intelligible only under
the application of the first half of the *Euthyphro* test – *viz.*, that
things are good for no other reason than that they are desired? For
if things are good, or of value, only because human beings happen
to like them, then there are no standards on the basis of which it is
objectively better for an individual to pursue one course rather
than another. Instead, it is merely a matter of what the individual
himself happens to want or prefer, there being no standards above
such personal inclinations and preferences. On this basis and
against this background, liberals and libertarians can insist that
"by nature" an individual is entirely free to choose this or that – in
other words, to do whatever he wants. Obviously, a freedom of this
sort is of no moral import whatever.

But enough of a characterization of the general philosophical setting appropriate to modern liberal individualism. What, then, may
be put forward as a setting appropriate to that alternative individualism that might be no less consonant with an individualistic
open society? Alas, here we find ourselves up against no little difficulty: for where in modern philosophy are examples of either a
moral or political philosophy that invokes the second part of the
Euthyphro test for its ethical first principles? (This is the part of
the test which says that things are to be desired only because they
are good, and hence not reckoned as being good merely because
they are desired.) The fashion in modern moral philosophy seems to
run entirely the other way: it just is not supposed any more that
men should pursue goals and objectives because they recognize
them to be truly good, and thus fit to be desired; no, it is so much
simpler to suppose that there really isn't any other reason to consider things good than that human beings tend to desire them. One
has but to run through the entire list of major moral and political
philosophers, from Hobbes and Locke right down into our own
Utilitarians, Libertarians, Equalitarians, *et al.*, and one will scarcely find anyone who even considers, much less is inclined to
subscribe to, what we might term a *moral* individualism based on
considerations of an objective good, towards which an individual
ought to aim. For this, one would presumably have to go back to
the Greeks, to Plato and Aristotle, or perhaps to St. Thomas in the

Middle Ages.

Perhaps it is not necessary to go quite so far back after all. For there is Richard Hooker, who lived in the sixteenth century – which is, significantly, the century before Hobbes and the great scientific revolution which had so disturbing an effect upon traditional philosophical notions of nature and of law. Hooker declares in his inimitable Tudor prose:

> All things that are, have some operation not violent or casual. Neither doth anything ever begin to exercise the same, without some pre-conceived end for which it worketh. And the end which it worketh for is not obtained, unless the work be also fit to obtain it by. For unto every end every operation will not serve. That which doth assign unto each thing the kind, that which doth moderate the force and power, that which doth appoint the form and measure of working, the same we term a *Law*.[7]

Nor would it have been in any way inapposite had Hooker added, "a natural law."

With this, we have a philosophical setting for the sort of individualism that might be a truly moral individualism, as contrasted with the individualism of liberalism or libertarianism. For one thing, on Hooker's account, the human individual is seen as being ordered by nature to a proper good or perfection which clearly meets the standard of the second part of the *Euthyphro* test, and which thus further qualifies as being man's natural end. Just as a plant, a fish, or any animal is ordered to its own proper perfection as the full-grown tree or fish or animal that it is by nature capable of being, so also a human being may be said to be ordered by its very nature to what may be conceived as being its proper perfection and fulfillment – *viz.*, its fully developed existence as a responsible and rational animal. This, in other words, is the sort of thing that a man's true good is, not merely because it is what men desire, but because it is what men ought to desire, and should pursue and bend their every effort to attain.

Similarly, as regards freedom, just as each and every thing in nature has "some pre-conceived end for which [that particular kind of thing] worketh" – an end determined by nature – so also human beings, so far from being bound by no law and hence free to do whatever they please, are rather bound by that very law which does

determine that very end or perfection toward which any human being is ordered by virtue of being human, and which therefore, as
Hooker says, "doth appoint the form and measure of [that thing's]
working" toward its own proper and natural end. Thus the freedom
of a human being is in no wise a freedom to do whatever one wants,
but is rather a moral freedom or freedom under law, in the sense
that a human being is free to make choices in accord with what his
reason and intelligence tell him he ought to do and be as a human
being, and what his responsibilities are for the living of his life. In
other words, this sort of thing could be called a moral freedom, as
opposed to a libertarian freedom that knows no law other than the
individual's own arbitrary whims and preferences.

Moreover, just as such a moral freedom, or freedom of intelligent
choice, is what underlies this "moral" individualism, so it should
now be clear how such a moral individualism should be the means
for salvaging the notion of a properly individualistic openness of
society, as well as the notion of individual rights within such a
society – without thereby committing ourselves to the various problems and enormities of a liberalism or a libertarian individualism.

Thus, for one thing, any libertarian individualism is supposed to
rest on the would-be moral basis of the individual's right to be free
and to do just as he likes, provided only that he not interfere with
others in their supposed equal freedom. But unhappily, there is no
such right, as we were at pains to point out earlier. As a consequence, there is no way in which a liberal or libertarian individualism can possibly provide a proper basis for individual
rights. On the other hand, in a moral individualism there is a basis
in nature for any individual to pursue his natural end. Why? Simply
because, as Aristotle and Aquinas would both argue, the good of
anything is simply definable as that thing's natural perfection or
fulfillment. Moreover, as a further principle, Aquinas lays it down
as the first principle of practical reason that *the good* of anything is
simply that which *ought to be pursued* or sought after by that
thing.[8]

And now for another thing: in our earlier criticisms of a libertarian kind of individualism, we found that, just as there could be
no justification of the supposed right of the individual simply to do
as he pleased, so also the attempt to correlate this right with a duty
to respect the similar right of others, or of those others to respect
the right of the first – this entire attempt to establish a consequent

pattern of reciprocal rights and duties has quite signally failed. But now consider the case of moral individualism. This time one begins with the well-grounded natural duty of each individual to be and become what he ought to be as a human person. That is to say, it is simply a natural moral duty of the human individual to make something of himself, in accordance with the requirements of his very perfection and natural end as a human being.

Moreover, be it further noted that such a duty – call it, if you will, a duty to self – is universal in that it is a duty incumbent upon every human being simply in virtue of his being human. In other words, it is universalizable as a duty of all men towards themselves. Notice further that any such duty on the part of an individual would seem inevitably to entail the possession of certain rights – and this on grounds not unlike that of Kant's famous principle that "ought" implies "can." For surely, if I am under obligation to carry out a certain task – say, that of preparing a certain report for my boss – then I can hardly be expected to do the job if my boss proceeds to encumber me with no end of other assignments that prevent me from ever getting to the business of my prior obligation to prepare the report. Accordingly, on this analogy, why may I not say that if, as a human individual, I am under moral obligation to make something of myself, and thus to become a rational and responsible person, then certainly I have the right not to be hindered in the discharge of this basic duty and responsibility? Specifically, it would seem that I would surely have a right to a certain freedom or liberty. There is no denying that living one's life, and living it well, as a responsible and accomplished moral agent, is very much a do-it-yourself job. No one else, no family, no society, no circle of friends, can ever do this job for one, or, as it were, program one to be a good man. No, I have to do it myself. What does this entail, if not a right to a certain freedom to figure things out for oneself, to make one's own decisions, and thus to learn for oneself what it is to be truly human?

If we but remind ourselves of those rights that would usually be cited as the distinctive stock-in-trade of any free and democratic society – the rights to life, liberty, and property – it must now also be clear that, just as I must have a certain liberty to live my own life and make my own decisions, so also I must have a right to the use of my own life and limb. Not only that, but if property be understood simply as such resources as I come to acquire in order, not just to keep body and sould together, but also to provide myself with opportunities for knowledge, human association, relaxation and so forth, then surely it would seem that I have a right both to try to acquire, and to dispose of, such needed material resources.

Remember that, like any other human being, I am one who in principle comes into the world bringing nothing with me. Hence, like everyone else, I have to concern myself with providing everything that is necessary, not just for life, but for the good life as well—food, clothing and shelter; knowledge, both theoretical and practical; association with other human beings, aesthetic enjoyment, religious devotion, etc. Surely, therefore, insofar as material resources are needed if I am to provide myself with these goods, I can be said to claim a right to such material resources and such means as I am able to acquire to this end.

But with this, might we not have provided a thoroughly justified foundation for an open society, understood in terms of an individualistic openness? For one thing, human individuals now have what can only be called natural duties and responsibilities, based on men's natural ends. Moreover, given such natural ends, as well as our natural human obligations to achieve such ends, it is possible to determine what our natural rights are—rights to freedom, to the disposition of our lives, our persons, and our property, etc., all of these being necessary means to achieve our proper perfection and flourishing. In other words, it is both warranted and morally necessary that human societies should be open societies, in the sense that as organized societies they represent human institutions, ordered to the end of providing such conditions as may make possible individual attainment of the true goals, natural perfections, and happiness of human beings. This is the open society that involves what we have termed a moral individualism, as contrasted with that undisciplined and morally unstructured individualism associated both with classical liberalism and with latter-day libertarianism. The weakness of liberalism need in no wise entail our having to forgo subscribing to an open society of the individualistic type. Instead, we need only recognize the true claims of a traditional natural-law type of philosophy and of ethics, and once again an individualistic open society can be reinstated and shown to have an adequate and proper philosophical foundation.

Notes

[1] Having earlier shied away from using a term like "the open society," on the ground that it does not seem to have any very precise meaning, how can I now compound the problem of imprecision by introducing terms like "liberal" and "libertarian," when no one is agreed as to what these terms mean, not even the liberals and libertarians themselves? My defense and apology for using such terms is that I urgently need a term to designate those who both traditionally and in the present day would be advocates of the sort of thing I am calling an "individualistic openness" in society; and certainly both liberals and libertarians would wish to be placed in that camp. At the same time, when it comes to the matter of the rather vexed differences between "liberals" and "libertarians," I will oversimplify this issue by appealing first to Locke's distinction between our human natural right to liberty, on the one hand, and our right to be treated as equals on the other. Then I will somewhat arbitrarily classify "libertarians" as being those who tend to uphold the right to liberty, at the same time that they are very chary about pushing for any such thing as a supposed human right to equality (Cf. Rothbard, Nozick, et al.). A present-day liberal, in contrast to libertarians and to those who are sometimes called classical liberals, tends to be one who pushes hard for men's supposed right to equality, even if it be at the cost of men's individual freedom and liberty.

[2] John Locke, Second Treatise of Government, ed. C.B. Macpherson (Indianapolis: Hackett Publishing Company, 1980), 8.

[3] Ibid.

[4] William Blackstone, Blackstone's Commentaries on the Laws of England, ed. Bernard C. Gavit (Washington, D.C.: Washington Laws Book Co., 1941), 68.

[5] For a precise statement of this principle, see William H. Frankena, Ethics, 2nd ed. (Englewood Cliffs, N.J.: Prentice-Hall, 1973), 25: "If one judges that X is right or good, then one is committed to judging that anything exactly like X, or like X in relevant respects, is right or good. Otherwise he has no business using the words."

[6] Jane Austen, Persuasion, in Johnson and Phelps, eds., The Novels and Letters of Jane Austen (New York and Philadelphia: Frank S. Holby, 1906), 1, 3.

[7] Richard Hooker, Of the Laws of Ecclesiastical Polity, ed. McGrade and Vickers (New York: St. Martin's Press, 1975), 109.

[8] St. Thomas Aquinas, Summa Theologiae, I-II, 94, 2.

Truth and the Open Society

James V. Schall, S.J.

It seems that certain things in this world simply cannot be discovered without extensive *experience*, be it personal or collective. . . .
— Alexander Solzhenitsyn

The disinterested pursuit of truth precedes all our theoretical and scientific tradition, including our tradition of philosophical and political thought.
— Hannah Arendt

To speak of science as a truth that man after many and long trials has grasped, will hardly sound attractive. . . . In a deep sense, science is not progressive. It is anchored in a few basic, nay metaphysical, propositions about the mind and the universe, just as philosophy is constantly pushed back to the same fundamentals.
— Stanley Jaki*

No doubt, the most fundamental passage in our literature about truth, as it is likewise the most famous passage about freedom, is found in the New Testament, almost in the form of a proclamation: "You shall know the truth, and the truth shall make you free." We can, thus, "know" things that are *not* true. We can know them as not true, or as seemingly true, even if they are not true. Only the former upholds the idea of truth. Truth lies in our judgment about *what is*. We read in *The Republic*, then, "Knowledge is presumably dependent on what *is*, to know of what *is* that it is and how it is."[1]

And truth is something that we *come to know*. We do not begin with it. Furthermore, we are so constituted that the seeking after the truth defines in some sense what is highest in us. Not without reason did Aristotle write early in his *Metaphysics*, surveying those who preceded him: "Let us review those who have preceded before us to the investigation of reality and who have practiced philosophy in the hope of discovering the truth."[2] The discovery of truth implies a truth-knowing faculty in each human being, a faculty which distinguishes him in the universe of material beings and makes of him an original source of openness to reality. It also implies the internal and external conditions which permit this faculty to operate "unrestrictively" before the world.

Yet, what is not true can be very persuasive. Truth clearly needs testing. The very first words of *The Apology* of Plato were these: "How you felt, gentlemen of Athens, when you heard my accusers, I don't know; but I – well, I nearly forgot who I was, they were so persuasive. Yet, as for truth – one might almost say they have spoken not one word of truth."[3] Socrates recognized that before his accusers, the truth was not likely to set him politically free. Speaking in the name of the philosopher before the city, then, Socrates, with a touch of regret, concluded:

> Do not be annoyed at my telling the truth; the fact is that no man in the world will come off safe who honestly opposes either you or any other multitude, and tries to hinder the many unjust and illegal doings in a state. It is necessary that one who really and truly fights for the right, if he is to survive even for a short time, shall act as a private man, not as a public man.[4]

The conflict of truth and polity is nowhere more clearly stated. The young man who witnessed the death of Socrates and who later went on to write *The Republic* suspected that the final city in which city and truth could exist would not be a city of this world.

No polity, it would seem then, can be truly "open" to the truth, so that the quiet of the private life is its only even temporary guarantee. Is this truth pursued in privacy, then, the truth that makes men free? Or, in other words, is final freedom not a product of polity at all? Socrates, like Paul and John, seemed to suggest that truth is something that can be both "known" and still rejected. Truth is not absolutely compelling as it is presented to us. This would suggest that the final roots of untruth are not in regime, but in will. No open society can guarantee the persuasiveness of *what is* to the judgment and will. No polity, then, will be immune from the effects of falsity, nor will any polity be able to locate in itself what is truth as such. A path to truth that is not political must be part of the civic good.

Aristotle had said that we begin with a mind, which mind distinguishes us from beings without this intellectual power. But we begin with a mind that does not "know" anything until it confronts, through the senses related directly to it in the human substance, what is not itself. All the mind knows as true, it comes to know. That is, the human being comes to know through his own intellect. And the human being knows directly what is not himself. Our own minds and selves are not known immediately, but they know in knowing something else that is not ourselves. We compare *what is* to what we know, to find their conformity or disconformity. It is in this act that we become aware reflectively of ourselves. Without beholding something else, we do not know that we are, or how we are.

The pursuit of knowledge begins with wonder, in the infinite variety of *what is*, not in doubt, to distinguish Aristotle from Descartes. This wonder is why, ultimately, we do not necessarily end up with only a knowledge of *what we make* – ourselves, in other words. Professor Leo Strauss described the difference between classical and modern political philosophy in these very terms:

> The fundamental change which we are trying to describe shows itself in the substitution of the 'rights of man' for 'the natural law': 'law' which prescribes duties has been replaced by 'rights,' and 'nature' has been replaced by 'man.' The rights of man are the moral equivalent of the *Ego cogitans*. The *Ego cogitans* has emancipated itself entirely from 'the tutelage of nature' and eventually refuses to obey any law which it has not originated in its entirety or to dedicate itself to any 'value' of which it does not know that it is its own creation.[5]

A knowledge of only ourselves is not a knowledge of the world which is not ourselves. It is not even an ideal. The newness of being to which we are open does not originate in us. We are beings who can delight in what is not ourselves. This is why we can accept that we are good, even if we are capable of doing what is not in fact good. The hypothesis that we are evil, which lies at the root of much modern political theory (Machiavelli, Hobbes), derives from methodologies, not from openness to being itself.

The Scriptural words about the relation of truth and freedom were not spoken in philosophic discourse. Rather, like Socrates, they were spoken by a Man who was finally executed, after a public trial, by religious and civil leaders, representatives of our highest traditions, whose authority even He recognized. One of these, the politician, was actually said to have inquired skeptically of the Man about to die, "What is truth?" This would suggest that politics is incapable of knowing truth, that it must persecute it any time it appears in public to demand presence. By different routes, Socrates and Christ arrived at the same place, where truth led to death in the polity. Both implied in different ways – immortality and resurrection – that no existing polity could or would be the location of the highest reaches of that truth to which man was open. Polity was not, thus, necessarily closed to truth except when it closed itself against the truth philosophy and revelation opened up before each human being in that being given to him. The substantial category of the individual human being always in the highest things transcended the relational category of the polity.

But while our tradition links freedom to truth, and truth to the Good, our "age," so to speak, seems to associate truth with the opposite of freedom. Pilate remains closer to our political regimes than either Socrates or Christ. We have come to use such words as "fascist" or "absolutist" to suggest that any articulated claim to truth – religious or philosophical – which claims our assent on the grounds of *what is*, constitutes, *ipso facto*, a threat to freedom. Truth, in this sense, does not make us free, but rather subjects us, deprives us of our freedom of permanent possibility.[7] Such "truth" cuts us off from the vast array of "non-truth," from the "not yet" both known and existing. What is not "true" might yet come to be true. We dare not cut our options off. What was false comes to be enforced by law within this or that regime. Peace depends upon the mutual tolerance of irreconcilables.

Society or culture, in particular, cannot survive on unchanging truths. The very claim to truth appears in politics, then, as necessitating the "closed" society. And while closed societies may be indeed successful, in the Machiavellian sense of continuing survival against other powers and other truths, they are feared evidently because they imply a stagnation or narrowness of scope, an exclusion of what "might" become true, including error. Yet, truth implies that some decision and distinction must be made. Some doctrines must be rejected. Some truths must be "self-evident" for a polity to be established. Not all things are possible, and not all that is possible is right. Dostoyevsky wrote that if God did not exist, all things are possible. Many of these "possible" things have come to pass, to our horror. Does this mean there is no God? Or does it rather mean that there is, that human evil, lest it be final, is an argument for God's existence?[8] Can a city be erected, in other words, open to what lies beyond its own evil? Is the problem of a deviant regime to be solved in exclusively political terms? Is the incapacity of the polity to close off evil and error the negative side of openness to truth, to the fact that since truth can be rejected, it can also be chosen and not fully existent until it is?

The "truth," then, suggests that in the modern era we need not think as we "must," to conform freely to *what is*, because it is. We relate ourselves to our own image, our political ideal, not because we have minds, from nature, but because we will what is to be true. We are obliged to nothing but ourselves, to our own subjective sincerity or authenticity. That is, this modern "truth" needs to conform to nothing but what is held, what is willed. We ourselves, therefore, must look upon will as limited by mere will, by itself, not by *what is*. Truth is not something intelligible we discover but did not make. We are the origins of our own "truth." "Truth" and "power" are thus interchangeable. Therefore, nothing can oblige us to be known simply because it exists apart from our own making. We constitute our own "truth." Leo Strauss described this issue in the following way:

> In modern times it came to be believed that it is wiser to assume that happiness does not have a definite meaning since different men, and even the same man at different times, have entirely different views on what constitutes happiness. Hence happiness or the highest good could no longer be the common good at which political society aims . . . . Hence the purpose of the individual and the purpose of political society are essentially different. Each individual strives for happiness as he understands happiness. . . . The public and the common is in the service of the merely private whatever the private may be, or the highest and ultimate purpose of the individual is merely private.[9]

Modern political theory is built precisely on this premise that the truth and the good have no possibility of resolution in *what is*. In the highest things, human beings are simply disparate.

Our regimes, moreover, are established on this basis. "Truth" is a private enterprise rather than a property of the common good to which each person is related as to something he is by nature open to. The "public" good is by definition, in the modern sense, constituted in name by the diversity of opinions claiming truth, themselves governed by the architectonic opinion which maintains that nothing is true (except this contradictory proposition itself). The "truth" is that the discovery of any truth undermines any established regime, so that civil peace and truth stand in opposition to one another. "Freedom" is, then, in this analysis, the consequence of the "untruth" established to order public things.

The "open society," in such a view, therefore, must be predicated upon the abiding unconcludability of "truth" discourses. Truth has no "status." It endangers the civil order in principle. "Error has no rights," but people in error do. This position sought to protect both truth and polity. Those "in error," however civilly legitimate, were still obliged to pursue truth as such, which truth transcended any existing regime. Yet, if philosophically "truth" means the theoretic rejection of its own possibility, the politician, subject to this theory and responsible for the regime based upon it, cannot simply avoid the practical consequences of the theoretic position. He must seek to establish, indeed, the "untruth" itself as the form of the regime, for its own safety. The philosopher must not only lead a private life and be silent, he must look upon his own truth-seeking faculty, what made him to be precisely the rational animal, as vain, if not actually a source of derangement and deception, as Descartes himself suspected. Those who dare to claim "truth," thus, are very dangerous. They threaten the foundations of any regime. Yet, those who "claim" truth can also be in error, so that a polity in which those in error can be challenged without fear to themselves or to those challenging them is a consequence of a regime which recognizes the worthiness of truth as such. Not all regimes need to be founded on the philosophical premise of theoretic skepticism.

Political philosophy, then, is related both to philosophy itself and to revelation (and indeed to poetry). The difference among actual regimes, symbolized by their enforced political frontiers in the modern world, constitutes the grounds upon which truth, both practical and theoretical, can be considered in civic freedom.

Socrates, in *The Apology*, insofar as he was a philosopher, though born in Athens, seems to have received his calling, his voice, from outside the actual polity in which he lived. The notion that there are some things all regimes ought to recognize as true, from reality, whatever the actual regime, the hypothesis of natural law, stands against the practice of those actual regimes which permit no "truth" other than what is upheld within their boundaries. But this position argues that, in the best regime, at least, truth and politics are compatible, though it is more than doubtful whether the "best" regime can exist in this world, but only in speech. This implies that the source and goal of truth are not ultimately political. Otherwise, all existing political foundations will seem to be merely "lies" or myths, in comparison to the fullness of "truth" itself. But this suggests too that an open society is not one in which "truth" is theoretically impossible, but only one in which openness to truth, whatever its source and end, be allowed to define the polity. This means that the political regime itself must have enough "openness" to truth to know the civil order's own limitations.

This openness to truth, however, which is not simply constituted by existing human will deciding what it wants, would necessitate some view about the definition and status of error, even in the best actual regime. Error means some disconformity between the human mind and a reality not constituted by this same mind. The problem, presumably, can be solved if we deny any status to truth. The best way to accomplish this is to interpret all truth as merely "opinion" and thereby, as we have seen, make democracy, in the Greek sense, to be simply the best regime. Democracy, in the classics, was the regime of freedom, in which to do what one wants constituted the end or purpose of the civil order. This position necessarily accommodated the welter of different views about truth, on the grounds that all truth is at best opinion. "Truths," as it were, not truth, exist. These truths or opinions can be contradictory because, and here lies the *political* importance of this thesis, men cannot be constantly at war with one another and still have opinions or ideas that are civilly, or even metaphysically, relevant. The ideas cause the wars, so that the only final solution is to control the ideas or reduce them to insignificance. The war of all against all is thus resolved, as Hobbes shrewdly explained, by power, not by open argument and persuasion, as Aquinas and Aristotle held. Legally, then, in this view, all truths must be reduced to opinions, and all opinions must be indiscriminately aired. All actual regimes are composed of only those opinions allowed to exist, or, to put it differently, no ideas about truth make any *public* difference. They can all exist or go on, provided they claim no establishment or resolution in the public order other than as their recognition of one opinion among many, even contradictory to others.

The only regime besides the best in which a Socrates could have survived, even for a spell, was a democracy of this sort. But he could survive not because the regime respected the philosopher or the truth, but rather because it could not tell the difference between truth and error, between the philosopher and the madman. Only when Socrates insisted on his vocation of dialectics, of rejecting at least some commonly held things in the city, things held by the poet, the craftsman, and the lawyer, before their sons, was he brought before the court as a threat to the particular regime so constituted to rule. Truth can survive in a democracy only if it is extremely modest, only if it is content to call itself in public "opinion." But perhaps if truth cannot survive as such in the polity, then its location may not actually be political. This question needs to be asked without implying that the political has absolutely nothing to do with the truth.

The inadequacy of the polity to define the truth, then, is presupposed to the openness to truth which is not mere opinion. The open society cannot be based on the theoretical skepticism of classical democracy (or its modern inheritors), but on the openness to those things which, however little known, are worth one's whole energies, as Aristotle taught at the end of the *Ethics*:

> But we must not follow those who advise us, being men, to think of human things, and, being mortal, of mortal things, but must, so far as we can, make ourselves immortal, and strain every nerve to live in accordance with the best thing in us; for even if it be small in bulk, much more does it in power and worth surpass everything.[10]

It is in the protection of this openness to the transcendent truth that the ultimate value of politics lies, even for itself. This alone is what can protect both truth from political deformation and protect politics from the temptation of itself constituting its own truth.

Aristotle left us with the heritage which warned that truth is not easy to come by. The open society must be seen not merely from the side of honesty, but also from the side of goodness and truth. We can be honest without yet having arrived at what is true. The burden of the true and the good, then, the fact that most men most of the time will be less than virtuous, the position of fact, in Aristotle's view, will ever make tempting a substitute metaphysics, which seeks to distribute truth and goodness to everyone by political means, means that do not arise immediately from character, reason, and will choosing the truth of *what is*. The latter fact, that our natural powers seem inadequate to know and choose the highest truth, was implied, at least, by Aristotle, when he suggested that "in many ways human nature is in bondage."[11] It is also, as Aquinas argued, one of the major arguments for an openness to revelation, itself addressed to a reason aware by its own powers of the human condition and its experienced difficulties, ones implied by the bondage about which Aristotle wondered.[12]

Eric Voegelin has suggested, furthermore, that the rejection of revelation leads, in today's intellectual atmosphere, not to a return to the condition of the classics before revelation (to Plato and Aristotle, as Strauss had hoped), which understood something of the fact of the corruption of nature in man and his limited openness to the transcendent, but to Gnosticism, to an imposition of self-derived truth and good as substitutes for the being in which alone human destiny and happiness are oriented.

> And the appearance of Christianity in history, with the resulting tension between reason and revelation, has profoundly affected the difficulties of philosophizing. . . . Today, just as two thousand years ago, *politike episteme* deals with questions that concern everyone and that everyone asks. Though different opinions are current in society today, its subject matter has not changed. Its method is still scientific analysis. And the prerequisite of analysis is still the perception of the order of being unto its origin in transcendent being, in particular, the loving openness of the soul to its transcendent ground of order.
>
> Only in one respect has the situation of political science changed . . . . There has emerged a phenomenon unknown to antiquity that permeates our modern societies so completely that its ubiquity scarcely leaves us any room to see it at all: the prohibition of questioning.[13]

The alternative to metaphysics and revelation, then, is not simply an open society premised upon theoretical skepticism or doubt, but a constructed "truth," an ideology, professing to explain how the chaos of opinions can be reduced to order.

The price of this alternative, the selection of ideology over *what is*, then, is, as Voegelin again put it, that we have people who know "why their opinions cannot stand up under critical analysis and who therefore make the prohibition of the examination of their premises part of their dogma."[14] The growing refusal to try tested, politically existing ideology against its own record cannot be explained simply by the Platonic notion of error as ignorance. The spiritual notions of pride and envy come into view precisely because of the inadequacy of reason alone before the evidence of what men do.

Following these insights of Voegelin, Dante Germino, in his *Political Philosophy and the Open Society*, endeavored, with much perception, to avoid the Gnostic danger of an ideologically closed society. At the same time, he sought to retain an openness to revelation and philosophy that could not be constrained by a civil law rooted in skepticism and freely chosen political forms, presupposed to nothing but themselves. For Germino, the widespread testimony of transcendent experiences, from many cultural sources, could not be excluded from the relevant evidence of what man is and what he is open to:

> In place of the term *open society*, which should be reserved for the spiritual reality of universal mankind, I propose that the term *opening society* be applied to those societies organized for action in the world that display the resources for periodic intellectual and spiritual renewal and the commitment in their laws, institutions, and traditions to the truth that humankind is more than a biological species. The opening society, despite its failings, affords a hearing to the philosopher and the prophet and to all others who witness to a truth that transcends the various idolatries of the day.[15]

What this requires, however, is some sort of test at this side of transcendence by which what arrives from openness, even from revelation, can be tested, at least by the principle of contradiction. Not every spirit is from the Lord. There is little doubt that the nearer we reach spirit, the nearer we are to deception, and this not merely from ourselves.

The citizens of Athens who accused Socrates of "atheism" were not easily moved by his defense that he did in fact believe in "spiritual things," therefore, he could not be an atheist.Whatever their crime regarding the philosopher, they were at least aware that spiritual things were also free things, so that the fact that something was spiritual did not yet prove that it was good or, especially, good for the polity. The classical function of philosophy, as Aquinas understood, was exactly that it addressed itself to this awareness.[16] But this works both ways. That is, sometimes it is quite "reasonable" to follow what seems beyond reason, that true spirits have the effect of increasing what is "reasonable." They do this, as known to the philosopher and the political philosopher, by addressing directly questions that have arisen, often poignantly, in the experience of reason and polity itself. This is why the death of Socrates and the death of Christ cannot be considered, as such, unrelated incidents.[17]

In a brilliant essay on the nature of much contemporary historiography, Gertrude Himmelfarb recounted the efforts to describe mankind from the position of mere "life," to ignore the difference it makes when man is also fully seen as a political animal. In this, Prof. Himmelfarb remains in full accord with Hannah Arendt, in *The Human Condition*, on this same tendency and its implications. In this more recent academic view, Prof. Himmelfarb pointed out, not the noble nor the good acts of mankind were what counted, not the city in which some reflection from the contemplative order was placed in the constitution and law, but rather ordinary, repetitive, indistinguishable "life" was to be the norm and function of human worth. Historiography has come to be a kind of salvation for the masses wherein immortality or resurrection is replaced by a massive volume detailing poverty and nutrition statistics. Thus, the "new history, in devaluing the political realm, devalues history itself."[18]

The openness to contemplation, in Aristotle's tradition, however, meant also the value and worth of politics as such, insofar as it knew and practiced the moral virtues, insofar as man rose above mere instinct and "life." Prof. Himmelfarb wrote:

> What they [social animals] do not have is a polity, a government of laws and institutions by means of which, and only by means of which, Aristotle believed, man consciously, rationally fulfills his distinctively human purpose, the 'good life.' The new historian, rejecting any such 'elitist' idea of the good life, seeking only to understand *any* life, in

fact regarding it as a triumph of the historical imagination to explore
the lowest depths of life, of unconscious, unreflective, irrational life,
denies that man is the distinctive, indeed unique, animal Aristotle
thought him to be – a rational animal, which is to say, a political
animal.[19]

The pursuit of pure freedom, of what each person does without
distinction with regard to truth or falsity, virtue or vice, the
democratic regime of the classics, does in fact leave us with a conception of man in which his rationality and polity are denied. An
open society, consequently, ought not to be opposed in theory to
one in which truth and order of virtue can likewise be recognized.

Several years ago, Leo Strauss remarked on a conference on the
good society which he was invited to attend. In his comments, he
rightly suggested why the question of truth and regime has become
especially a question for "ex-believers." The crisis of the open society is really an issue of subjectivity, the replacing of "wonder" by the
"self" as the location of truth. A society based in the latter, in the
self, will, subsequently, have no "guidance," as Strauss put it, but
itself. The open society will not be possible to this view because it
has denied the nature of that faculty, the reason, which opens men
to what is not themselves.

Prof. Strauss wrote, then, to this point:

> Not a few people who have come to despair of the possibility of a de-
> cent secularist society, without having been induced by their despair
> to question secularism as such, escape into the self and into art. The
> 'self' is obviously a descendant of the soul; that is, it is not the soul.
> The soul may be responsible for its being good or bad, but it is not
> responsible for its being a soul; of the self, on the other hand, it is not
> certain whether it is not a self by virtue of its own effort. The soul is a
> part of an order which does not originate in the soul; of the self it is
> not certain whether it is a part of an order which does not originate in
> the self. Surely the self as understood by the people in question is
> sovereign or does not defer to anything higher than itself; yet it is no
> longer exhilarated by the sense of a state of despair. . . . I believe that
> one should admit the fact that the unbelief in question (in the modern
> world) is in no sense pagan, but shows at every point that it is the
> unbelief of men who or whose parents were Christians and Jews.
> They are haunted men. Deferring to nothing higher than their selves,
> they lack guidance. They lack thought and discipline. Instead, they
> have what they call sincerity. Whether sincerity as they understand it

is necessary must be left open until one knows whether sincerity is inseparable from shamelessness. . . .[20]

Sincerity, as I have suggested elsewhere, is "the most dangerous virtue" because it gives all the external aspects of truth but based in itself, not in the objective reality.[21] Sincerity is the deviation from the good and the true, from *what is* to what is felt ought to be true. Finally, it substitutes the latter feeling for the substance of truth itself.

The refusal to believe in the truth, locating it rather in the *will* than in *what is*, likewise, is a theme recurring in John's Gospel. Hannah Arendt too had elaborated the fragility of practical truth, the record of fact and evidence that could be distorted by tyranny and fear.[22] Jeane Kirkpatrick added to this, following Solzhenitsyn and Orwell, that the refusal to believe in the evidence of deep tyranny, excusable perhaps for those directly subject to terror or torture, is more a characteristic of many in free democratic societies of the modern world, citizens who do not have the excuse of coercion to prevent their seeing the truth.

> Ours is probably the most violent century in history, and still we cling to pale euphemisms and blind theories of inevitable human progress. The will to disbelieve the horrible is, I believe, a defining characteristic of the contemporary West, of no society more than our own. Because we cannot remember the fact of danger, we have great trouble protecting ourselves, our freedom and civilization. But the persistence of the horrible is only one of the lessons we are unwilling to learn. Almost as strong as the will to disbelieve the shackling of freedom imposed on society after society by our only major contemporary adversary, is the will to disbelieve our own worthiness. The will to disbelieve that we value freedom and intend to expand and preserve it, has been translated into an expectation that we are almost always wrong.[23]

We do not merely have the need to write "in secret" because of our political condition, of which Strauss spoke, but we have an unwillingness to speak and accept the truth, theoretical or practical, when we are told of it contrary to our ideological presuppositions. In this sense, truth, the careful recounting of *what is*, the essence of practical intelligence and action, is not corrected by any society, however open.

"Open societies," George Will has also written in this regard, "frequently have difficulty comprehending regimes of radically different character."[24] What needs to be stressed, however, is that this difficulty seems rooted not so much in the openness as such of society but rather in the theoretical justification for it. This is a conception of truth which cannot on any intellectual grounds really explain why closed societies are not correct, perhaps even superior, since they know their own standards. Without a metaphysics, open societies seem uncertain before their own rejection in the name of a truth which is grounded only in will, in ideology itself, since the latter is at least whole and consistent with itself because it is formed in its own image.

Aristotle, in his *Metaphysics*, recalled the essential contrast with this position by his reminder that the human mind is open to what is not itself:

> The human mind, or rather the mind of any composite being, does not possess the good at this or that particular moment, but attains the best of things – which is something other than itself – over a whole period.[25]

It is this persistent realization that the human intellect is open to what is not itself that guarantees freedom *from* the demands of the individual and collective self-will that forms its own image on which to impose, by power or propaganda, its vision on men.

"Though we are active when judging and claiming, at the end," Paul Weiss wrote, "we are receptive, awaiting support and perhaps correction by objective appearances and actualities."[26] The moderation of political philosophy is, then, justified because of its own understanding that it is not itself a metaphysics. And yet, the question can be asked not only about the limits of politics but about the limits of metaphysics. The open society requires leisure and a contemplative stance which permit the questions that arise within it to be reflected upon according to all the voices and words that are spoken, all the deeds enacted in its midst, but spoken and acted with the solidity of philosophy and political, practical virtue within the polity.

The end of the open society, however, ought not to be conceived as simply a public order, or even a correct metaphysics, however transcendent to civil life itself. The seriousness with which political philosophy takes the questions of happiness, friendship, virtue, and goodness that arise within its own pursuit, questions that take political and ethical philosophy to philosophy itself, do not seek, or at least do not find, their end or perfection in a polity. Aristotle's questions in his discussions of friendship remain central to political philosophy because their lack of adequate philosophic answer leaves the polity open to the temptation of providing its own substitute for them. Thus Aristotle observed that "when one party is removed to a great distance, as God is, the possibility of friendship ceases."[27] The second question is this:

> For existence is good to the virtuous man, and each man wishes himself what is good, while no one chooses to possess the whole world if he has first to become someone else (for that matter, even now God possesses the good); he wishes for this only on condition of being whatever he is. . . .[28]

Such questions, insoluble by philosophy or political life as such, whether we would wish really for some happiness other than that for our particular selves in our uniqueness, or whether we can be friends with God since friendship seems to be of the perfection of higher being, are questions that first arise in ethical and political philosophy, in discovering what it means for man to be a political animal. They lead naturally, logically, suasively to an ultimate openness to which intellectual creatures are receptive, to which they are receivers, not makers.

To recall the remarks of Eric Voegelin cited earlier, even scientific analysis is in some sense based on a spirit of openness to being, to *what is*, and its origin. The human soul, the human person needs to remain open, receptive in a loving way to its "transcendent ground of order." Josef Pieper, it seems, reformulated the force of this position in this manner:

> Even in Christian theology, the highest form of *caritas* is defined as loving God as *the dispenser of bliss*. But bliss, which is ultimately sought in all love, is nothing but the final quenching of the deepest thirst. Man is by nature a thirsting and needy being – not only, as Kant said, insofar as he 'belongs to the world of sense,' but also and especially insofar as he is spirit. It is not in our power to be so 'unselfish' that we can renounce the ultimate quenching of our thirst, bliss. We *cannot* want not to be blissful.[29]

The two essential points to which Aristotle as a political philosopher and metaphysician leads us, to questions that are insoluble within the polity, to which he always ascribes only a "secondary" happiness, namely, that of friendship with God and that of each individual's possession of the highest happiness as such, for *himself*, are the very ones with which revelation is most concerned.

The question posed from political philosophy, then, is not whether any open society can receive or institutionalize such revelational responses to such questions, but rather whether the sorts of human beings for whom such questions seem insoluble are to be permitted and encouraged to live according to answers that do in fact correspond with the questions as asked by philosophy, itself a check on revelation's authenticity. The end of Prof. Strauss's discussion of the *Politics* of Aristotle is as follows:

> In asserting that man transcends the city, Aristotle agrees with the liberalism of the modern age. Yet he differs from that liberalism by limiting this transcendence only to the highest in man. Man transcends the city only by pursuing true happiness, not by pursuing happiness however understood.[30]

The openness to truth as such, not just the openness to any truth, is what defines ultimately our freedom.

In this sense, then, the regimes of this world, existing regimes, are not the location of what is best in us. Our regimes can deceive us, as we can deceive ourselves. But the very moderation of the best practical regimes, based on the awareness of what they are not, is testimony to the seriousness with which the answers to the highest questions are to be taken by the human city. It is no accident that we can classify regimes according to the degree they deviate from the truth and the good. Some really are worse than others. This is the truth. Truth, however, remains at its best the end of the open society. The skeptical roots of modern liberalism, to give it credit, are the only alternative to political philosophy. And this skeptical alternative leads with inexorable logic in practice to ideology and universal tyranny somehow, to the very opposite of the truth, to the willing of the worst even with evidence.

Man is indeed a "thirsting and needy being" especially insofar as he be spirit. Political philosophy exists to understand how the aspects of man which are not spirit lead to the final happiness to which he is ordained as a whole. Philosophy, contemplation, teaches us what is spirit, what we must ask of *what is*. The open society is a collection of our answers. Revelation, finally, poses at least one set of answers to the questions rising from within political life and philosophy, a set of answers directed at the same truth, directed at the same philosophizing person in whom the questions have arisen in the first place.

In the end, then, we need not know the truth, nor need we choose to be free. This is the root of our curious dignity. This is, however, also why the contrary choice to acknowledge the truth and choose the good can properly arise from political life, from political philosophy, from philosophy itself, open each in some fundamental sense to *what is*. We can, perhaps, leave the final word about the open society to Plato, from whom the whole question, no doubt, began in the first place:

> And we say that this tendency [of mathematics and reality itself to make it easier to know the 'good'] is possessed by everything that compels the soul to turn around to the region inhabited by the happiest part of *what is*, which is what the soul must by all means see.[31]

In conclusion, what is compelling about the truth as about the good is *what is* itself, for its own sake. We can hardly blame Plato for his insistence that we ought not miss the highest things, if we wish to be what we are, first receivers even of the highest things.

Notes

* Alexander Solzhenitsyn, "Foreword," in Igor Shafarevitch, *The Socialist Phenomenon* (New York: Harper, 1980), vii; Hannah Arendt, *Between Past and Future* (New York: Viking Press, 1968), 262-63; Stanley Jaki, *The Road of Science and the Ways to God* (Chicago: University of Chicago Press, 1978), 327.

[1] Plato, *Republic* V.478a.

[2] Aristotle, *Metaphysics* 983b3-4.

[3] Plato, *Apology* 17a.

[4] Ibid., 32a.

[5] Leo Strauss, *The City and Man* (Chicago: University of Chicago Press, 1964), 44-45.

[6] See James V. Schall, *The Politics of Heaven and Hell: Christian Themes from Classical, Medieval, and Modern Political Philosophy* (Lanham, Md.: University Press of America, 1984), 235-52. See also J.M. Bochenski, *Philosophy—An Introduction* (New York: Harper Torchbooks, 1972), 93-101.

[7] See Schall, "Possibilities and Madness: A Note on the Scope of Political Theory," *The Review of Politics* 37 (April, 1975): 161-74.

[8] See Schall, *The Politics of Heaven and Hell*, 107-28.

[9] Strauss, *The City and Man*, 31-32.

[10] Aristotle, *Ethics* 1177b31-78a2.

[11] Aristotle, *Metaphysics* 982b29.

[12] See Schall, "The Supernatural Destiny of Man," *Modern Age* 26 (Summer/Fall 1982): 411-15; review of Ralph McInerny's *St. Thomas Aquinas* in *Teaching Political Science* 10 (Summer 1983): 195-98; and "Political Philosophy and Christianity," *Center Journal* 2 (Fall 1983): 47-66.

[13] Eric Voegelin, *Science, Politics, and Gnosticism* (Chicago: Regnery-Gateway, 1968), 21.

[14] Ibid., 22.

[15] Dante Germino, *Political Philosophy and the Open Society* (Baton Rouge: Louisiana State University Press, 1982), 182.

[16] St. Thomas Aquinas, *Summa Theologiae* I,1, ad 2: "Unde nihil prohibet de eiusdem rebus, de quibus philosophicae disciplinae tractant secundum quod sunt cognoscibilia lumine naturalis rationis, et aliam scientiam tractare secundum quod cognoscuntur lumine divinae revelationis." See also *Summa Theologiae* I,114,1-5 for Aquinas' discussion of how spiritual beings can lead to evil and how a knowledge of moral good is properly something in control of the human will.

[17] See Schall, *The Politics of Heaven and Hell*, 21-38.

[18] Gertrude Himmelfarb, "Denigrating the Rule of Reason," *Harper's* (April, 1984): 87.

[19] Ibid., 90.

[20] Strauss, *Liberalism: Ancient and Modern* (New York: Basic Books, 1968), 261-62.

[21] Schall, *The Praise of 'Sons of Bitches': On the Worship of God by Fallen Men* (Slough, England: St. Paul Publications, 1978), 53-62.

[22] Hannah Arendt, *Between Past and Future* (New York: Viking, 1968), 227-64.

[23] Jeane Kirkpatrick, Address at the Hoover Institution Dinner, Washington, D.C., January 10, 1984.

[24] George F. Will, *The Pursuit of Virtue and Other Tory Notions* (New York: Simon & Schuster, 1982), 16.

[25] Aristotle, *Metaphysics* 1075a7.

[26] Paul Weiss, *First Considerations* (Carbondale: Southern Illinois University Press, 1977), 36.

[27] Aristotle, *Ethics* 1159a4-5.

[28] Ibid., 1166a19-22.

[29] Josef Pieper, *Enthusiasm and the Divine Madness*, trans. R. and C. Winston (New York: Harcourt, 1964), 96.

[30] Strauss, *The City and Man*, 49.

[31] Plato, *Republic* VII.526e.

Order in Nature and Society: Open or Specific?

Stanley L. Jaki

It is an old truth that the present, which is the father of the future, is also the child of the past. At any moment man, individually and collectively, is in transit from past to future. Nobody would challenge the fact that there is a very instructive history behind the great confrontation which today splits the globe into two camps. Liberals and regimenters (socialists) began to make history well over a century ago and some of their writings have become the kind of classics against which latter-day liberals and socialists (regimenters) measure their originality or the lack of it.

An historian of science can bring a special perspective to this great confrontation and its origins. One need only recall the resolve of the followers of J.S. Mill or Karl Marx. They all tried to appear scientific as they argued the respective measure of liberty and regimentation, then as now the chief bone of contention. J.S. Mill discoursed on political liberty on the basis of a vast study of logic and scientific method. The measure of that vastness was coextensive with the universe. He found grist for his mill of liberalism even in the evolution of solar systems and galaxies. Few paragraphs in his prolific writings give a more telling glimpse of the nature of the liberalism he preached than the one in which he spoke of remote areas of the universe where two and two do not necessarily make four.[1] This suggests that behind the aversion to constraint, so characteristic of liberalist politics and economics, there may lurk a view of the universe in which anything can happen and allegedly does happen. Such a state of affairs, it may be noted in passing, reflects a radical multiplicity, a multiverse, which is the very opposite to a thoroughgoing coordination of things and processes within a coherent framework, or to the converging of all into a unity, a uni-verse in short.

The view that anything can and will happen, that there are no strict boundaries and forms, that everything is in flux, received in Mill's time further support in Darwin's theory. Darwin loved to return to the notion of chance, to the image of an unspecified primordial cosmic soup, out of which by some strange accidents there arose, after a long chain of unpredictable turns, our present flora and fauna—an unlikely offshoot of the past and an unforeseeable matrix of the future. Not surprisingly, Herbert Spencer, who coined the phrase "struggle for survival," also articulated a cosmic philosophy based on the tenet that anything could happen. The universe of Spencer was a multiverse both in space and in time. From a hypothetically complete or *almost* complete homogeneity he tried to derive a most specific and fully coordinated state of affairs—our universe—which in turn was to dissolve itself into a nondescript homogeneity. From it there would arise another, wholly unpredictable cosmic situation.[2] As is well known, Spencer had his greatest vogue in America, where more than one captain of industry, a Rockefeller, a Carnegie, and others, saw in Darwinian science a carte blanche for an industrial struggle in which the only certain thing was that the stronger would devour the weaker.[3] So much for the background which a historian of science may provide about the scientific underpinnings of the so-called liberal outlook on life. That outlook implies the least amount of restraint in human interactions, because interaction among physical entities all across the cosmos is supposed to proceed along ever variable patterns.

No less strong was the confidence with which the opposite camp, or the spokesmen of strict social regimentation, felt their program and creed to have been steeped in science. In the preface to the second edition of *Das Kapital*, Karl Marx made it all too clear that the laws of society as derived from the tools of production were meant by him to be as exact as the laws of physics.[4] This is not to suggest that Marx knew more than a smattering of physics, although less than a hundred years ago anyone with a moderate scientific inclination could gain a fairly good grasp of physics if he applied himself seriously for a year or two. Unfortunately for Marx, his chief consultant in matters scientific, Friedrich Engels, remained woefully ignorant of physics, his prolific discourse on it notwithstanding. That not only application but also scientific frame of mind may have been in short supply in Engels' case should be clear to any unbiased reader of Engels' *Dialectics of Nature*, which became a canonical writing for party ideologues concerning the interpretation of science.[5] But the *Dialectics of Nature* leaves no doubt about Engels' conviction that Marxism was a strictly scientific theory.

This connection between science and socio-economic theory aiming at strict regimentation is no less clear in an undeservedly forgotten Marxist classic, the *Eternité par les astres*, written in 1871 in a most fearsome French prison, the island fortress of Taureau off the port town of Morlaix in Brittany.[6] Its author was none other than Louis Auguste Blanqui, Marx's chief antagonist for the leadership in the First International. Part of the antagonism may have been derived from Marx's realization of Blanqui's superiority as a speaker, thinker, and activist. It is indeed difficult not to admire the sweep with which Blanqui elaborated on strict cosmic determinism, which would produce through eternity the recurrence in an infinite number of times of exactly the same configurations, physical conflicts as well as individual and social struggle. In spite of all his sweep and consistency, Blanqui did not face up to the problem of why there should be any struggle in a fully deterministic existence, let alone the problem of why there should be a free and purposeful call for struggle if everything was fully determined. He chose to dodge the question of freedom, a perennial source of nightmare for advocates of complete individual and social determinism.

The consistency with which Blanqui and other regimenters of society swept under the rug the question of freedom has an additional instructiveness. It is related to the question of the use of science as viewed by social theorists, be they the advocates of unrestrained liberalism or of strict regimentation, or, to use contemporary clichés, of an open or of a closed society. Around 1870 there was unanimity concerning the strictly determined nature of physical interactions. Almost all those who supported the notion of causality in physical interaction rested their case on the strict determinacy implied in the Newtonian laws of physics. The most graphic and memorable statement of causality in all physical processes came at that time from none other than T.H. Huxley, as he reminisced on the first reactions to Darwin's theory. Huxley had particularly in mind the objection which dismissed the Darwinian mechanism of evolution as a reign of pure chance, the very opposite of what mechanism ought to be. Natural selection and Darwinism as a whole were, Huxley argued, the very opposite to the reign of chance, because they were science and science could not tolerate chance events. While the subtle hereditary changes and the interaction of the environment with the organism could elude exact observation in most cases, the situation there was no different from the splashing of waves against rocky shores:

> The man of science knows that here, as everywhere, perfect order is manifested; that not a curve of the waves, not a note in the howling chorus, not a rainbow glint on a bubble which is other than a necessary consequence of the ascertained laws of nature; and that with sufficient knowledge of the conditions competent physico-mathematical skill could account for, and indeed predict every one of those "chance" events.[7]

This beautiful declaration was the embellished echo of Laplace's famous passage about a superior spirit who, being in possession of all parameters of all bodies at a given instant, could calculate and predict every future situation.[8] Laplace, it is well to recall, carefully avoided any reference to human freedom. He most likely would have revolted at the thought that his dicta on that superior spirit were the outcome of an ironclad necessity. Huxley would have protested in the same way against the inference that his and Darwin's scientific works, or any discovery made by any scientist, was a foregone conclusion, an inevitable outcome of upbringing, education, or, to mince no words, of the whirl of molecules within the brain and the brawn.

How is it then that the same deterministic Newtonian science gave rise to two very different social philosophies: one aiming at unlimited freedom, the other at the practical absence of any freedom at all? The answer to this question helps to understand not only the historical antecedents of the present-day conflict but also the true measure of science behind the actual conflict itself. The liberals—a J.S. Mill, a Spencer—had in view more than science taken in a strict technical sense. They rather entertained a picture of Western intellectual history in which science, or rather its rise in the seventeenth and eighteenth centuries, coincided with and presupposed the liberation of human reason from transcendental shackles, superstitions at worst, metaphysical dreams at best. This picture received its hallowed codification in Condorcet's *Essay on the Progress of the Human Mind*[9] and became a staple fare of education through the influence of Comte's positivism. In other words, science meant for those liberals much more than its technical contents and methodological precepts with which they were often unfamiliar. Science for them represented above all a state of mind unfettered by any presupposition, a state of mind open to all possibilities, and a mental attitude aiming at maximum behavioral freedom.

In the opposite camp, the camp of strict social regimentation, the emphasis was on the content of science, on its alleged witness that everything, including human behavior, individual and social, was strictly determined. The historical context of the rise of science was in that camp ascribed not to a new mentality but to the industrial conditions, which necessarily formed the frame of mind needed for doing science. Not surprisingly, the cultivation of science within that camp had to be subject to organizational control. Long before Lenin achieved political power, he called for a sustained vigilance over science as well as scientists.[10] His call was a loud echo of the voice of social Utopians, aptly called the Prophets of Paris, of whom Fourier and especially Comte thought up astounding ways of putting science into a strait-jacket lest the cultivation of science encourage aspirations for intellectual freedom. The enslavement of science became a reality whenever the proletariat could set up its dictatorship. An ideology, which ascribed the chief cause that moulded human society to social organization, could only be hostile to Mendelian genetics, which left no room for the dream that the socialist behavior of the revolutionary generation would be inherited by subsequent generations. Lysenkoism was not the only example of party dictatorship over science. Brain research and neurology had to suffer no less serious setbacks, once the Pavlovian reflex theory was imposed in the name of dialectical materialism. The cultivation of cosmology, relativistic physics, and quantum theory also had to suffer. Tellingly enough, this dictatorship over science was relaxed only when, in the early 1950s, Soviet physicists told the Party that they could not produce the scientifically sophisticated tools needed by modern warfare unless their research was not interfered with by Party ideologues.

About the time when Lenin tried to harness science for the program of social regimentation, and free-for-all capitalism looked for support in the evolutionary science of Spencer and Darwin, there appeared Bergson's *Evolution créatrice*, a heroic effort to vindicate for human freedom a more than verbal meaning.[11] That Bergson suspected nothing of the coming of social regimentation on a vast scale, that is, the turning of Marxism into statehood, should be of no concern here, revealing as it is of the short-sightedness of a penetrating mind. As the product of a typically Western bourgeois milieu, Bergson focused on Cartesian (Newtonian) mechanism and on its Spencerian-Darwinian extension to biology. He certainly made a stir by forcefully reminding his generation of the point made long before him that no novelty can occur in a universe conceived in terms of mechanistic physics. Yet every change, even mere physical change, implies novelty and this is certainly true of biological processes, to say nothing of mental and volitional experiences. All these are taking place in time, the perennial wellspring of novelty. While Bergson's emphasis on time as primary matrix could call for serious qualifications, for our purposes it should be sufficient to note its fundamental role in Bergson's philosophy, which being that of a great thinker was a philosophy of cosmic range. It was not only about things, organisms, and persons that Bergson stressed the fact of their endurance across time. He emphatically noted, by using italics, that "the universe *endures*."[12] This cosmic endurance immersed in the flow of time was for Bergson the reason for an endless rise of novelties in each and every context. He went so far in emphasizing the unique character of all such novelties as to speak of continuous creation through which the future becomes so novel that its prediction on the basis of the past and present is, to quote his words, "a veritable absurdity."[13]

Bergson had, of course, to lay great store by biology, in which he found a storehouse of refutations of ironclad mechanism. Biology was far less in view when, twenty-five years after the publication of the *Evolution créatrice*, he published its sequel, *Les deux sources de la morale et de la religion*. There, in trying to vindicate the evidence of novelty in social evolution, he made much of the notion of an open society as opposed to a closed one. The latter was rooted in the instinct of self-preservation, individual and tribal, the former in altruism, which Bergson saw best exemplified in the love preached and practiced by Christ. About the reason for the emergence of Christian love at a specific point in the historical evolution of humanity, Bergson stayed with generalities. His ultimate appeal was to the universe as a mysteriously living entity with a quality of life well-nigh divine. He saw the entire universe "peopled with intentions,"[14] all of which were groping toward something divine as they became conscious in man whose ultimate responsibility was to "fulfill. . . the essential function of the universe which is a machine for the making of gods."[15] Such was the grand conclusion of *Les deux sources*, which went through seventeen editions in only three years, an appropriate indication of the impact, very transitory to be sure, it had made.

Bergson's universe, the foundation of open society, was certainly open – it was, indeed, wide open to any and all novelty, including the ones that hardly fitted into his cosmic optimism tainted with pantheism. Revealingly enough, his account of the universe was void of specifics. Thus, one would look in vain in Bergson's two main works for any specific norm or precept which would impose itself on humanity in the sense which is the case with a law of nature or, rather, with a natural law. The only sense in which Bergson was specific was negative, namely, his courageous criticism of such opponents of free development as dictatorial regimes. Freedom of action and of thought he certainly wanted to preserve even at the price of risking his own security. But he laid down no norms in terms of which mankind should face up to overpopulation, in Bergson's opinion the greatest threat to human survival.[16]

Bergson's avoidance of specifics about his open society and the rules governing it, an avoidance which is certainly of a piece with the lack of specific contours in his notion of the universe, is all the more curious because he was not unfamiliar with the startling developments in physics during the first three decades of the century. Bearing witness are the questions he posed as Einstein faced a distinguished audience at the Sorbonne on April 6, 1922.[17] Bergson may have sensed that although modern physics more than amply discredited classical physics (or rather the mechanistic materialism often taken for it), which certainly excluded novelty, the advent of a new physics was a threat in disguise to his cosmic view of an unspecified and interminable novelty or openness. For as modern physical science grew by leaps and bounds, each subsequent advance unfolded aspects of the universe which show it to be not so much indefinitely open as distinctly specific. As any specific entity, the universe too is therefore definitely limited to a very finite number of future possibilities or novelties.

Modern physical science had quickly become the prey of that two-fold exploitation in the hands of liberals and regimenters which had already befallen classical or Newtonian physics. Modern, or twentieth-century, physics added a new perspective, however, to the dispute between the two camps and also a new standard by which both are to be judged. This holds true also of a third way, which created no less stir than did Bergson's and which owed much to Bergson's at times rather poetical philosophizing.

The new perspective is related to quantum mechanics, or the mathematical method which deals with the enormously vast and crucial range of atomic, nuclear, and subnuclear phenomena. The word quantum, although it appeared in various meanings here and there in philosophical and scientific literature well before 1900,[18] came into its own historic role in that year with a paper which Planck presented to the Berlin Academy. In that paper Planck argued that a most fundamental type of radiation, called black-body radiation, cannot be accounted for unless one assumed that the emission of radiation took place in discrete units or quanta. During the next quarter of a century every major advance in atomic physics brought further evidence on behalf of Planck's claim. Indeed, that progress brought to the fore much more than Planck originally envisioned, although he suspected from the start the philosophical thrust of further progress in quantum theory. Around 1925 Heisenberg discovered that the calculation of energy differences between spectral lines called for a mathematical technique called matrix calculus. A strange technique indeed, which implies that on the atomic level one must work not with ordinary algebra but with a non-commutative algebra in which x multiplied by y is not necessarily equal to y multiplied by x. In other words, on the atomic and subatomic levels conjugate variables, or pairs of certain physical parameters, such as distance and velocity, position and momentum, time and energy, obey rules with consequences anything but ordinary. The most important of these, enunciated by Heisenberg in 1927, states that the simultaneous measurement of such pairs implies an uncertainty at least as large as Planck's quantum.

Heisenberg's uncertainty principle has since become a cultural matrix. A recent example of this is an essay in *Time* following the almost fatal shootings of President Reagan and Pope John Paul II. The narrow escape of both was in the eyes of many a miracle, an act of Providence, a view which, the essayist argued, was above scientific objection because for science all events are ultimately chance occurrences.[19] But the essayist's understanding of chance, whatever else might be said of it, has no foundations in quantum mechanics or its underlying philosophy. What he would find, if he looked, is that its formulators are bogged down in an equivocation which is the result of their failure to distinguish between two propositions: one states the limited measure of man's ability to measure exactly, either in theory or in practice, a physical interaction; the other states that because exact measurement of an interaction is impossible, the interaction itself is inexact in the sense that the effect can contain more than what is contained in its cause; that is, the effect is not caused fully, and may not be caused at all. The first of these statements is purely operational, the second is radically ontological. To suggest that the first implies the second is sheer equivocation, the result of an elementary mishandling of the laws of logic.[20] It would not be tolerated in any moderately good freshman course untainted with that modal or subjective logic which Hegel grafted on to modern thought. Yet this equivocation or logical fallacy has become part and parcel of our modern scientific culture. There the notion of chance has grown, soon after Heisenberg's enunciation of the uncertainty principle, into the basic dogma of anti-ontology. In that culture the real is replaced by the unreal garbed in the cloak of chance. While for the unwary that garb means only the absence of exact measurement, for the "initiated" it is a specious cover-up for a situation in which the real does not necessarily need to rest on anything real. The real becomes in the end a mere appearance, to the delight of phenomenologists, who forget their initial resolve to make no utterance whatever about reality as such.[21] Hence the rise of the widespread belief, amounting to a climate of opinion, that anything can happen and that man therefore is not bound by anything specific such as natural law, which obviously presupposes a specific ontological order.

Such is the allegedly scientific foundation of the notion of "open society" which, in post-Bergsonian times, had Karl Popper as its chief ideologue through his *The Open Society and Its Enemies*.[22] Indeed, in arguing against universal determinism as invoked by "closed" Marxist regimes, Popper made much of quantum indeterminacy.[23] Confident that he had thereby deprived Marxism of its scientific basis, he felt free to point his finger at the Messianic or religious inspiration of Marxism. For an avowed rationalist like Popper the chief threat to his "open society," which he carefully distinguished from the one advocated by Bergson,[24] had to reside in religion. And since only one religion, Roman Catholicism, stood persistently for the rationality of religion even when implying the supernatural, a careful reader of *The Open Society and Its Enemies* could not help feeling that his real target was neither Plato, nor Hegel, nor Marx, nor Hitler, but the Catholic Church, for which Popper voiced only contempt, though with careful indirectness, by heaping scorn on the Middle Ages.[25] Such was, however, a deft and accurate strategy, as only during the Middle Ages did there arise a broadly shared conviction that existence and its norms were very specific, since the universe owed its existence to a Creator who could have brought forth an infinite number of worlds, all very specifically different from one another.[26] In that conviction, actual creation and actual cosmic specificity were two sides of one coin.

In the 1980s, when we see Western society disintegrating in more than one respect, it should seem clear that the rationalism of the Enlightenment, which liberated man from supernatural constraints, brought about a frightening kind of openness. It is the openness of a barrel casting off its hoops and losing all its contents, an openness in which all norms, even purely pragmatic and essentially biological norms, are brazenly dispensed with. Suffice it to recall the recognition of lesbian and homosexual couples as legally married units, an outcome which fills with foreboding even diehard rationalists and professional pragmatists. They cannot help but recognize both the biological indispensability of "normal" marriage and the Church as its only consistent defender.[27] The real enemies of open society are not societies based on absolute and even on supernatural revealed truths, but the ideas of intellectual circles that opted for chance as the ultimate. Such an option is fallacious to the point of pushing to the brink that modern open society whose real strength lies in its inherited capital of absolute truths and values on which it has been thriving as a parasite.

Ideas are more dangerous than weapons. The latter may or may not be used. Ideas – the history of philosophy, theology, and of political theories shows this all too well – run their courses inexorably. It was no accident that, say, Fichte's works were readily available in field libraries of German armies. The hundreds of millions of copies in which the ideas of Stalin and Mao were made available were very effective in sparking bloodthirsty purges and marches of madness. By the same token, an ideology which claims, even if on the basis of science, that anything can happen, will inevitably invite anarchy. Distinctly anarchical are several symptoms of Western society which, following the rejection of traditional constraints, have spread all over during the last thirty years.

As one would expect, spokesmen for Marxist regimes and ideologies fought tooth and nail against this scientific abolition of ontological causality in the name of quantum mechanics, or rather of its Copenhagen interpretation. It was not unexpected, either, that their own defense of causality had to be counterproductive. Being an offshoot of Hegelian dialectics, Marxist realism could never see reality for what it is. Partly because of this, the defense of causality in Marxist realms bogged down in its efforts to revindicate Newtonian determinism or, rather, the possibility of exact measurements. Freedom, of course, remains a nightmare within Marxist realms in more than one way. It is, however, no less nightmarish to find some well-meaning Western scientists arguing that the Heisenberg indeterminacy principle provides a narrow margin within which freedom can operate. Few of these scientists are so clear-headed as was Eddington, the first to propose such a defense of freedom and also the first to recognize that it was sheer nonsense.[28] It is well to recall that if the questioning of freedom is not to become a begging of the question itself, it cannot cast doubt on the freedom of raising that very question.

So much for the new perspective which twentieth-century science gave to the question of freedom. Once again, as was the case a hundred years ago, philosophical and valuational presuppositions prevailing within a society, that is, in its ideological matrix, could play a much more important role than the science available to that society.

The same may not be true with respect to another major development in twentieth-century science, which, as has been previously suggested, may play the role of a standard against which debates about the measure of freedom, or rather the openness or closedness of society, should be evaluated. This other scientific development is not yet a quarter of a century old. It was only in 1963 that a strange radiation was observed in the Bell Telephone laboratories in Holmsdale, N.J. The radiation has since become famous under the name of the 2.7°K cosmic background radiation. All too often, and very wrongly, this radiation is presented in the literature, technical and popular, as something which gives the age of the universe; nay, something which puts us at the threshhold of creation.[29]

The 2.7°K radiation is extremely valuable for a reason which, for better or for worse, has already been dubbed the anthropic principle.[30] In plain scientific terms the 2.7°K radiation proves two things. One is that the universe was smaller and smaller as its history is traced further and further into the past. This is an independent confirmation of the expansion of the universe which has been known for about fifty years, although some scientists kept doubting that the red shift in the spectrum of galaxies was really a proof of their recessional velocity. Further doubts on that score are hardly permissible. The other thing proved by the 2.7°K background radiation concerns theories about the formation of the elements, theories first proposed in the 1950s. According to these theories, the formation of chemical elements from hydrogen through helium to carbon and to the still heavier elements could take place only if about 15 billion years ago all matter in the universe was contained within a volume not larger than a planet, a volume in rapid expansion. Furthermore, all matter in that phase (lasting for much of the first three minutes of cosmic evolution) had to consist of protons, neutrons, and electrons, together with 40 million photons for each of these particles. Such a mixture had a specific pressure (and temperature) which provided a specifically needed rate of expansion against the gravitational force.

Since 1963, enormous scientific work has been done on this very early phase and on earlier and even shorter phases of the universe, with a result which invariably has the same thrust as a stark philosophical message. The message is that we human beings are part of an immensely specific and coherent state of affairs, which involves the entire universe. That there is a universe may be a trivial statement, though not for those who are aware of the claim of all post-Humean and post-Kantian philosophies that the idea of the universe is merely a bastard product of the metaphysical cravings of the intellect. In this age, which has achieved for the first time in history a truly scientific grasp of the universe, the Kantian position about the universe cannot be openly maintained by "scientific" philosophers, whatever their vested interest in that position which undermines the rationality of looking at the universe as a jumping board to its Creator. The avoidance of the notion of the universe on the part of professedly "scientific" philosophers should seem therefore most revealing. One would look in vain for a non-trivial reflection on the *reality* of the universe (the totality of consistently interacting things) in Popper's latest book, *The Open Universe*, which contains a mere page on what has been revealed by modern scientific cosmology about the universe.[31] No less characteristically, Popper did his dialectical best to make the status of the big bang theory appear "very precarious," although it alone explains the 2.7 °K background radiation which Popper did not find worth mentioning. As late as 1982, Popper still was resting his case on half-century-old equivocations about indeterminacy which would never give rise to permanent specificities, let alone to those very specific features which, as unveiled by modern scientific cosmology about the universe, should overpower a truly open intellect. On the contrary, modern scientific cosmology overpowers the speculative intellect by unveiling a universe with very specific features. Indeed, precisely because those features are so specific, they discourage attempts to consider them to be the mere creations of the mind. Only a most self-centered thinker would claim that the existence of ten billion and one protons for every ten billion antiprotons is necessary on a priori grounds. Yet such a specific ratio is required if 40 million photons, or units of electromagnetic radiation, should be available during the first ten-thousandth of a second for each proton, neutron, and electron, so that the cooking of chemical elements, mentioned above, may get under way.

One of these elements is carbon, the very basis of life as we know it. It is the element which forms the backbone of organic chemistry and, in that sense, of human life as well. Whatever its marvelous range of properties, carbon has become a commonplace even for organic chemists. Yet even in itself carbon should be a cause for

wonder because it is a most specific construct. Around no other element can the theoretical chemist build a world as variegated as
around carbon. One only need recall speculations about silicon-
based life, which some dreamy-eyed cosmologists present as alternative forms of life in outer space, to realize that in this regard
silicon is a poor second to carbon, to say nothing of other elements
of the Mendeleev table. Our admiration for carbon should know no
bounds when we realize that a whole universe of very specific subnuclear particles and very specific forces ruling them was
necessary to produce carbon. Indeed, the cosmic cooking process
followed a most specific recipe, prescribing second after second
every step of the process, which in fact could have lasted for only
about three short minutes some 15 billion years ago.

Such is the scientific basis of the so-called anthropic principle.
Since we humans, so many anthropoids, are made of carbon, it appears to many modern cosmologists that the universe was made for
the sake of man, that is, for a purpose. They could have, of course,
taken any element in order to reach the same conclusion. They
could indeed have taken the blueness of the sky, the average size of
a mountain, the average size of a star. These and many other very
ordinary aspects of the universe have their explanation in a most
specific coordination of all constituent parts of the universe. This
coordination, startling in itself, becomes the more astonishing the
further we trace its properties back in time.

When a scientist, marvelling at this extraordinary state of affairs, begins to suspect that such a specificity indicates a designer,
and therefore a purpose, he merely shows himself a poor
philosopher, a Johnny-come-lately kind of wisdom lover. If a scientist fails to recognize that his scientific work is a proof of purpose,
his marvelling at cosmic purpose, or anthropic principle, will not
produce noteworthy results. This is why so many cosmologists slide
from the anthropic principle to the worst kind of anthropocen-
trism, which is the solipsism of idealist philosophy for which only
the ego exists.[32] A realist can hardly do more with idealists, be they
scientists, than wish them well. One has to be on guard, however,
against the perennial snare of idealism. Even the slightest cavort-
ing with it can deprive one of the sense of reality without which any
discussion about the measure of freedom will run out in trivialities,
at best, or in sheer willfulness, individual and regimented, at its
very rawest.

About the willfulness of regimented society little needs to be said, except (to remain with my topic) in the form of a brief reference to the suspicion under which the science of cosmology is kept by Marxist regimes. It is clearly realized in those realms that modern scientific cosmology, by presenting us with an enormously specific universe, almost becomes a first chapter in theology, a chapter on Creator and creation. Consequently, the respective measure of freedom and law in human society becomes a metaphysical issue, a prospect which can hardly be tolerated within Marxism, whether it be cruelly institutionalized or the humane kind still dreamed about by some academics in the West. This, of course, holds true also of the so-called open society which in the Western world has so many spokesmen, many of whom mean openness in a distinctly anti-theological sense. To argue with them on theological or metaphysical grounds is entirely futile. Nor can one argue against them with reference to natural law. They would answer in derision that many Christians, nay Catholics (especially among these the self-styled Thomists of the transcendental kind), are cutting their own throats with the very scalpel with which they dissect natural law. But against these champions of an open universe and against some of their unwitting allies one can effectively argue in the name of science. In science they believe, and therefore they must be open to a discourse about the vistas opened up by such a commonplace element as carbon. Carbon can indeed be turned into heaps of hot coals on the heads of spokesmen of an openness according to which, since everything is possible, everything should be tried out because all constraints are artificial, purely man-made.

The anthropic principle, or let us state less metaphysically, the very scientific carbon principle, shows exactly the opposite, namely, that very few things are possible. If one takes three or four constants – the speed of light, the radius of an atom, the charge of an electron, the mass of a proton – then one can show that the sky can only be blue, a mountain can never be higher than ten miles, and a star never one hundred times heavier or ten times lighter than our sun.[33] If one says carbon and if one knows what goes into the cosmic production of carbon (indeed the whole cosmos goes into it), one has stated a very narrow track for a carefully engineered cosmic engine which runs its course on a very specific timetable. Clearly, far from everything should be considered possible in a universe in which stars and planets would have never evolved if the total mass of the universe had differed by a mere one percent from the one which actually does exist. The claim about the openness of the universe is a subtly disguised claim that the universe is fuzzy, that is, undetermined in its very foundations. It is on that claim about cosmic fuzziness that rests the further claim that it is unscientific to speak either of law or of freedom, let alone of an objectively proper relationship between liberty and constraint. Whatever the universe of some philosophers, the universe of science is the very opposite of that fuzziness which underlies the doctrine of the so-called open society in a so-called open universe.

The art of determining the objective proportion of constraint and liberty does not belong to science but to metaphysics, ethics, and theology. The art in question is not even the domain of that jurisprudence which readily reinterprets a constitution steeped in natural law according to the dictates of the latest Gallup poll. The relatively little and indirect contribution which science can make to that art must not, however, be belittled. Whether we like it or not, we live in an age of science. Science has become a currency which is universally accepted and looked for. The value of that currency is hardly ever questioned in a broad and systematic sense. Warnings about the limitations of its value are often intemperate. Moderate voices are not given a public hearing, let alone sufficient publicity. Truth, unfortunately, cannot compete with half-truths in newsworthiness. One need not therefore expect a sudden change in the climate of opinion, even if there developed a wider awareness about the enormous degree of lawfulness, specificity, and coherence in the universe from atoms to galaxies and beyond.

To grasp the significance of that enormous degree of specificity, which with all its exactness is embedded in reality, one should resort to philosophical tools more penetrating than phenomenology, however intuitive, can provide. The tools of the latter remain ineffective for the purpose even when wrapped in biological terms, as was the case with Bergson, or in terms of evolutionary paleontology as articulated by Teilhard de Chardin, who wanted to inject new life into the Bergsonian approach. Thus, whatever Fr. Teilhard's intentions, he only made palatable in some Catholic circles, to which his influence was largely reduced, the view that man was after all but a product of nature. Against a purely naturalistic explanation of man, so fashionable in this age of science, one can and must however stress that precisely because of scientific reasons, man cannot be less specific an entity than is the universe. The best and most exact in science suggests indeed that mankind, no less than the universe, has been put on an extremely narrow track. Traditionally speaking, that narrow track conjures up natural law which cannot be defended if it cannot be shown that nature is most specifically lawful. This is not to suggest that there is much cogency in the merry galloping of, say, an Edmund Burke who, in one and the same sentence, went from the laws of commerce through the laws of nature to the laws of God.[34] The real situation is much more complex than Burke's statement would have us believe. But reality is not so complex as to be that sophisticated chaos in which anything is falsifiable except, of course, the principle of falsifiability.

To be sure, reality, as described by modern science, evidences a great deal of openness to novelty. Unlike the mechanistic universe, in which novelty was impossible, the universe as described by modern science goes through specifically successive stages, each with a predominance of features which could not come about in any of the preceding or subsequent stages.[35] In that sense our universe, a most specific universe, is a place for novelties but never in the sense which is tantamount to somersaults in logic. Science cannot justify the somersault according to which something evolves out of something which is not there. Nor does science justify the kind of mental acrobatics which glibly assure us of the rise of life of non-living matter and of the emergence of consciousness out of mere sensitive life. The apparently dinosauric touch of this latter claim may suddenly appear very modern, or avant-garde, if one recalls a warning made recently from a scientifically most prestigious post. Sir Andrew Huxley, president of the Royal Society and a great grandson of T.H. Huxley, can hardly be suspected of hostility toward a so-called evolutionary openness, the basis of claims that man can take his destiny, his measure of freedom and constraints, in his own hands. Yet Sir Andrew stated in his Presidential Address nothing less than that science offers only speculations about the origin of life, and as regards the problem of the origin of consciousness, Darwinists by and large preferred to sweep it under the carpet.[36]

If, however, such is the case, nothing can stand seriously in the way of the only true openness available for man. It is the openness of his contingent being toward its very ground which is the Creator's free act. In that act, specific laws and free choice were simultaneously given to man. Today no less than before, man must have both. Otherwise he will be the slave of a communal willfulness which blocks his view of the past, ruins his present, and deprives him of any future worth looking for.

Notes

[1] For details and documentation, see my Gifford Lectures, *The Road of Science and the Ways to God* (Chicago: University of Chicago Press, 1978), 151.

[2] Spencer's cosmology received its most concise and devastating indictment from none other than H.G. Wells, who in book I, "Metaphysics," of his *First and Last Things: A Confession of Faith and Rule of Life*, definitive ed. (London: Watts & Co., 1929) wrote: "He [Spencer] believed that individuality (heterogeneity) was and is an evolutionary product from an original homogeneity, begotten by folding and multiplying and dividing and twisting it, and still fundamentally *it*" (30).

[3] The standard account is *Social Darwinism in American Thought*, rev. ed. (Boston: Beacon Press, 1955).

[4] See Marx's preface to the second edition of *Capital*, translated from the third German edition by S. Moore and E. Aveling (New York: Appleton, 1889), xxx-xxxi.

[5] A fact all the more reprehensible because by 1928, when the manuscript of the Engels book was published, not only was physical science vastly beyond the physics of the 1870s and 1880s, which Engels had in view, but his analysis of it was all too often utterly amateurish.

[6] For details, see my *Science and Creation: From Eternal Cycles to an Oscillating Universe* (Edinburgh: Scottish Academic Press, 1974), 314-19.

[7] Huxley's statement is from his reminiscences on the reception of Darwin's *Origin of Species*; see F. Darwin, ed., *The Life and Letters of Charles Darwin* (New York: Basic Books, 1959), 1:553-55.

[8] Or as Laplace put it in the introduction to his *Essai philosophique sur les probabilités* (1814), the human mind was but a feeble outline of a hypothetical intelligence "which would comprehend all the forces by which

nature is animated and the respective situation of the beings who compose it – an intelligence sufficiently vast to submit these data to analysis – it would embrace in the same formula the movements of the greatest bodies of the universe and those of the lightest atom; for it, nothing would be uncertain and the future, as the past would be present to its eyes." See *A Philosophical Essay on Probabilities*, trans. F.W. Truscott and F.L. Emory (New York: Dover, 1951), 4.

[9] For details, see my Fremantle Lectures (Balliol College, Oxford), *The Origin of Science and the Science of Its Origin* (Chicago: Regnery-Gateway, 1978), 30-31.

[10] Lenin did so in 1908 in his *Materialism and Empirio-Criticism* (New York: International Publishers, 1927), 323-24.

[11] First published in 1907. Henri Bergson, *Creative Evolution*, trans. A. Mitchell (New York: Modern Library, 1944).

[12] *Creative Evolution*, 14.

[13] Ibid., 371-76.

[14] Bergson, *The Two Sources of Morality and Religion*, trans. R. Ashley Audra and Cloudesley Brereton (Garden City, N.Y.: Doubleday & Co., 1954), 163.

[15] Ibid., 317.

[16] Ibid., 290.

[17] Those questions related to the reality of simultaneity and to the validity and fundamental character of common-sense knowledge. On both accounts Einstein kept repeating, rather evasively from the philosopher's viewpoint, that he viewed those questions only from the perspective of the operationist method of the physicist. The full transcript of Bergson's long questions and of Einstein's answers is the concluding part of the question-answer period that followed Einstein's lecture on relativity before the *Société française de philosophie* on April 6, 1922; see its *Bulletin* 17 (1922): 91-113. That Maritain was present at that lecture is clearly shown by a passage in his *Distinguish to Unite; or The Degrees of Knowledge* (New York: Charles Scribner's Sons, 1959), 158, where Einstein's resolve to consider only the operationist aspect is pointedly recalled: "Listening to Mr. Einstein lecturing on simultaneity, it was very remarkable to hear him constantly returning to the question: what does the word 'simultaneity' mean for me, a physicist?" For further details, see my "Maritain and Science," *The New Scholasticism* 58 (1984): 267-92.

[18] As shown by the long list of examples in *The Oxford English Dictionary*, vol. 8 (Oxford: Clarendon Press, 1933). In that list, obviously completed a few years before its printing, no reference is yet contained to the use of quantum in modern physics, a use very much established by 1920! Not mentioned in that list is a prominent use of the word quantum, namely, a long chapter "Quantum" in Hegel's *Science of Logic*, trans. W.H. Johnston and

L.G. Struthers (London: George Allen & Unwin, 1929), 1:217-332.

[19] *Time*, 27 April 1981: 79.

[20] For further details, see my "Chance or Reality: Interaction in Nature versus Measurement in Physics," *Philosophia* 10-11 (1980-81): 85-105.

[21] That the deceptiveness of that unintended "anti-ontology" is even greater than that of its fully conscious Cartesian counterpart was forcefully recalled by Maritain in his *The Peasant of the Garonne*, trans. M. Cuddihy and E. Hughes (New York: Macmillan, 1969), 124-39.

[22] First published in 1943. Karl Popper, *The Open Society and Its Enemies*, 5th ed. rev. in 2 vols. (Princeton: Princeton University Press, 1966).

[23] Ibid., 2:85.

[24] See the long opening note to the Introduction, 1:202-03.

[25] See ibid., 2:24-25 and 303.

[26] The first to point this out was Pierre Duhem, who did it on an astonishingly vast scale in his pioneering researches on the medieval origins of modern science, especially in his Leonardo studies and his 10 vol. *Système du monde*. For details, see "Duhem, the Historian" in my *Uneasy Genius: The Life and Work of Pierre Duhem* (Dordrecht: Martinus Nijhoff, 1984), ch. 10.

[27] See *Time*, 13 December 1982: 74.

[28] See Eddington's *The Philosophy of Physical Science* (London: Macmillan, 1939), 182, for his repudiation of what he had stated in his *The New Pathways of Science* (Cambridge: University Press, 1935), 88.

[29] In that respect, there is something subtly misleading in the very title of S. Weinberg's most informative and very readable book, *The First Three Minutes: A Modern View of the Origin of the Universe* (London: André Deutsch, 1977).

[30] For an excellent semi-technical account of that principle, see B.J. Carr, "On the Origin, Evolution and Purpose of the Physical Universe," *The Irish Astronomical Journal* 15 (1982): 237-53. For a corrective of the philosophical statements made by Carr, see my article, "From Scientific Cosmology to a Created Universe," ibid., 253-62.

[31] Karl R. Popper, *The Open Universe: An Argument for Indeterminism* (Totowa, N.J.: Rowman and Littlefield, 1982), 143.

[32] I have heard solipsist views endorsed, in the presence of fairly large gatherings, by such distinguished astronomers as McCrea and Sandage. Well-known for his solipsistic proclivities was, of course, Eddington.

[33] For a not overly technical account, see F. Weisskopf, "Of Atoms, Mountains and Stars: A Study in Qualitative Physics," *Science* 187 (1975): 605-12.

[34] While Burke was right in doing so, for instance, in his impeachment speeches against Warren Hastings of the East India Company, who flouted elementary honesty in his rulings (see Burke's *Works*, 1827 ed., 16:165-66),

most specific laws of commerce, such as interest and depreciation rates, have little if anything to do with natural law, let alone with the laws of God. [35] Thus, for instance, the translational, vibrational, and rotational degrees of freedom of a molecule can be activated only in a way which does not correspond to a straight ascending line (representing the continuous increase of heat input), but along phases which follow one another as ever higher plateaus. Much the same happens in the evolution of the cosmos, where the steady drop of temperature permits the activation of similar successive plateaus, corresponding to the formation of distinctly new configurations, ranging from subatomic particles, through atoms and molecules, to galaxies, and within the latter, to stars and planets. Herein lies the source of novelty with respect to purely material entities and not in some quasi-mystical indeterminacy, which ultimately pre-empts of its unique status that source of specific novelty which is man's free will and creativity.

[36] See *Supplement to Royal Society News*, iss. 12, Nov. 1981: v.

Democracy and the Open Society

Dante Germino

Contemporary writing about democracy in American political science tends to exhibit two main defects. The first of these has to do with the overemphasis upon democracy's pragmatic aspect to the neglect of its symbolic dimension. The second, which is related to the first, concerns the need to link democracy to a theory of universal mankind as an "open society."

One has only to place the writings of Plato beside those of Machiavelli, Hobbes, and Locke to grasp the magnitude of the shift towards literalism in the modern political consciousness. Plato's language suggests far more than it contains: rich in myth and allegory, it opens out to the vision of the transcendent *agathon*. Machiavelli, Hobbes, and Locke, on the other hand, narrow the focus of human concerns. Machiavelli wants to strip away symbolic "adornments" to present the "effective truth of the matter." While he is interested in more than power (esteem for the dimension of "glory" sets him apart from his English successors), it is man the power-seeker rather than man the God-seeker who is at the center of his preoccupations. In Hobbes and Locke, the social contract metaphor prevails. No better example could be found of the shift from the symbolic to the literal consciousness than the rise to predominance of the social contract metaphor, explicitly rejected by Plato's Socrates in the *Republic* as an example of *doxa* (opinion) as opposed to *episteme* (knowledge). Politics is then on the road to becoming the science of "who gets what, when, and how," or what C.B. Macpherson has more elegantly described as a theory of "possessive individualism."

Macpherson argues persuasively that the doctrine known today as "pluralism" is a variety of possessive individualism. To use Antonio Gramsci's terminology, one may describe pluralism as the "hegemonic" idea of democracy at the present time. In Macpherson's words, this pluralism, reflected in the work of Truman, Dahl, Schumpeter, Almond, Verba, and others, holds that

> the current system of competing parties and pressure groups does perform, as well as possible, the democratic function of equilibrating the diverse and shifting demands for political goods with the available supply, and producing the set of political decisions most agreeable to, or least disagreeable to, the whole lot of diverse individual demands. This empirical pluralism is based on an economic market model: the party leaders are the entrepreneurs, the voters are the consumers. The voter's function is not to decide on policies but. . . to choose one set of politicians who are authorized to decide the policies. This function does not require, nor does it permit, widespread continuous citizen participation. The system is lauded for its efficiency in maintaining equilibrium in providing some degree of consumer sovereignty. Its function is not to promote individual self-development but to meet the demands that individuals, as maximizing consumers, actually have and are able to express.[1]

Macpherson goes on in the article from which the above quotation is taken to offer his own version of what he calls "participatory democracy." Participatory democracy takes the fulfillment of human needs rather than "system-stability" for its "overriding value." It encourages individuals and groups that have been pushed to the margins of society to demand recognition of their needs and desires. Philosophically speaking, participatory democracy recognizes the human condition to be one of change and development. Human nature has both an "historical" and an "ontological" dimension. Participatory democracy, Macpherson continues to argue, seeks to develop a democratic pluralism, a pluralism represented most profoundly in Marx's "humanism." Participatory democracy engages in a radical critique of capitalism; its theorists claim to demonstrate that a truly democratic order and the capitalist economic system are incompatible with each other. Participatory democracy aims to overcome "alienated labor" and to replace it with unalienated labor – defined as labor "in the broadest sense – creative transformation of nature and of oneself and one's relations with one's fellows." Such unalienated labor was recognized by Marx to be *"the* truly *human* need."[2]

Having taken Macpherson's summaries of both the "mainstream" theory of democracy and that of its "radical" critics as a starting point, let me proceed to Henri Bergson's discussion of democracy in *The Two Sources of Morality and Religion.* My reasons for bringing in Bergson are twofold: he was the first thinker to use the term "open society," which I contend is essential to an adequate theory of democracy; and he shows an appreciation for the fact that, above all, democracy is a *symbol.* It points beyond any claimed embodiment of itself. Democracy is at its core a spiritual force. Although pragmatic machinery for determining how governmental leaders are selected, cashiered, and replaced is an obvious necessity, such machinery alone cannot guarantee democracy. Democracy's motive power must come from its ethos, from the psychological dispositions predominant in its citizenry.

In selecting Bergson's characterization of democracy as an example of an alternative theory to either the radical or mainstream conceptions prevalent in American political science today, I hardly mean to endorse all that he says; I have elsewhere criticized Bergson's political and moral thought for its "activist mysticism."[3] What I do contend is that in his remarks on democracy in the *Two Sources,* Bergson conveys something essential that is missing from the regnant pluralist model: *viz.,* democracy's spirit, *élan,* and expansive power. Bergson understood that above all, modern democracy is a faith that moves human beings, a faith whose roots go far back into Western history. Here are his words:

> Of all political conceptions, [democracy]. . . is the only one to transcend, at least in intention, the conditions of the "closed society." It confers on man inviolable rights. These rights. . . demand of all men an incorruptible fidelity to duty. It therefore takes for its matter an ideal man, who respects others as he does himself, inserting himself into obligations which he holds to be absolute, making them coincide so closely with this absolute that it is no longer possible to say whether it is the duty that confers the right or the right which imposes the duty. The citizen thus defined is both "law-maker and sub-

ject," as Kant has it. The citizens as a whole, the people, are therefore
sovereign. Such is democracy in theory. It proclaims liberty,
demands equality, and reconciles those two hostile sisters by reminding them that they are sisters, by exalting above everything fraternity. Looked at from this angle, the republican motto shows that the
third term dispels the oft-noted contradiction between the two
others, and that the essential thing is fraternity: a fact which would
make it possible to say that democracy is evangelical in essence and
that its motive power is love.[4]

Undoubtedly one hears here a version of democracy with a heavy
French accent. There is in it a good deal to which American
pluralism would object, especially the Rousseau-like invocation of
the "sovereignty" of the people.[5] Even if one grants that Bergson's
formulation of democracy is vulnerable to pragmatic dissection
both by "elite" theorists (Mosca, Dorso) and by American pluralist
political scientists, the fact remains that he reveals modern
democracy's symbolic dimension in a way in which the theorists of
elites and of pluralism do not. Indeed, one may ask whether it is appropriate to apply the standards of pragmatic, instrumental reason
to what in context is clearly a poetic, symbolic evocation.

"Democracy is evangelical in essence." If Bergson's dramatic
words are to be understood properly, they must be placed in the
context of his distinction between the "open" and "closed" morality.
The closed morality is the morality of pressure, exclusivity, and, indeed "possessiveness." The open morality is the morality of aspira-
tion, universality, and a surrender of self to the open society, the
universal community of the spirit that transcends any visible
power organization.[6] When Bergson insists that democracy is
"evangelical in essence," he means to say that in conception at
least, democracy originates in the open morality of the Gospels and
above all the Sermon on the Mount. Democracy's motto is also that
of Augustine: "Love, and do what you will."

To the obvious objection that almost two millennia separate the
proclamation of the open morality in the Gospels and the American
Declaration of Independence and the French Declaration of the
Rights of Man, Bergson responds that the hold of the closed morality, so congenial to our primal "nature," was so strong that it took
many centuries for the open morality to penetrate and leaven the
political thinking of the West. When it finally did so, it was in a

secularized form, and the religious origins of democracy were obscured by the language of "the rights of man."

A cynical rejoinder to Bergson's characterization of democracy's essence would be easy. "What has love to do with politics?" say the "political realists." I suggest, however, that Bergson's poetry explains democracy's perennial appeal better than do either of the current theories of pluralism and radicalism. Would people risk their lives, fortunes, and sacred honor for "polyarchy"?

The great American documents of democracy, from Thomas Jefferson's *Declaration of Independence* to Lincoln's *Gettysburg Address* to the Atlantic Charter of Roosevelt and Churchill and the United Nations Declaration of Human Rights, may not be dismissed as mere froth. If they do not speak Bergson's language in all respects, they nonetheless burn with a passion, a moral commitment, a universality lacking in today's pragmatic accounts of the struggle for power and advantage for one's group or interest.

Macpherson argues that the radical theory of "participatory democracy" shows the direction in which society must go to overcome possessive individualism (or what Bergson called the "closed morality"). However, I find it difficult to understand how it would do so. Bringing groups and individuals hitherto left out of the scramble for power and advantage into the political arena, where they must be reckoned with on pragmatic grounds, extends pluralism's reach; it does not constitute a critique of possessive individualism. Indeed, the result of more energetic, better organized participation by the citizenry in politics might be an increase of possessive individualism and not its diminution or overcoming.

Looked at purely on its own terms, "participatory democracy" does nothing to challenge the ethic of acquisitiveness itself. I see no reason to believe that anything fundamental would change in a participatory, as opposed to a passively pluralist, democracy. Unless preceded and accompanied by a change of consciousness, or spiritual *metanoia*, the change of economic structures (from a capitalist to a socialist economy, for example) would not result in a democracy that moved human beings in the sense of the great documents already cited.

Enabling those presently among the *emarginati* (an Italian word for those pushed to the side in the race for power and wealth) to obtain recognition and dignity is in itself an aim worthy of democracy in the Bergsonian sense. Without a *metanoia* on the part of the groups at the center, however, the *emarginati* will continue to be in the position of second-class citizens.

A fully developed theory of democracy must be grounded on a fully developed theory of the human being. As an Indian political scientist, Raghuveer Singh, recently observed:

> Everybody would agree that politics is concerned with human life. It makes no sense to talk of politics of atoms and molecules, of cats and rats, of oaks and rocks. Yet the question remains, what is human life? Is it life in the sense of sheer bio-physical existence, or the satisfaction of material needs, of desires and wants? Or is it life in terms of its quality, meaning and purpose? Even rationality cannot be said to be a differentia of human beings, for even highly developed self-propelled mechanisms, computers and robots are also possessed of intelligence and rationality in some sense. Man must be defined by his reflective self-consciousness, by his awareness of his own self and non-self and by his understanding of his own nature and destiny. In other words, he must have the capacity for self-consciousness and self-transcendence. His temporal existence can only be understood in terms of eternity, his own self in terms of a transcendental self. Politics which is concerned with man's relations with his fellow be-ings is devoid of meaning except as seen *sub specie aeternitatis*. It is not just any kind of relation among human beings that we are con-cerned with in politics. We are concerned with ideal relations, or with the real quality of these relations. People living under what Rene Guenon aptly described as the 'reign of quantity' and obsessed with the purely factual character of reality scarcely realize that without quality no conception of reality is possible.[7]

Professor Singh goes on to say that a fully developed theory of the person is "conspicuous by its absence" from mainstream Western political science, whether one considers it in its "behavioral" or "post-behavioral" manifestations. Nor can the "humanist-critical-Marxist, existential-phenomenological or analytical linguistic framework" provide such a theory, for, although in some ways superior to the "scientistic paradigm," such a framework is an intellectual mess. As Alisdair MacIntire has shown in his recent book *After Virtue*, contemporary philosophy has been reduced to propaganda by the various competing wills to power on the intellectual scene.

One promising exit from the debacle is to return to Henri

Bergson and to explicate his theory of the "open society" as it has been revised and philosophically strengthened by Eric Voegelin. A fully developed theory of the person emerges from such an approach. Furthermore, it has the advantage of overcoming the parochialism of Plato and Aristotle. Rather than being an exercise in nostalgia for an idealized past, such a theory is open to new evidence pertaining to the process of political reality.

In the *Declaration of Independence*, Thomas Jefferson wrote that "all men are created equal." These words are usually taken to apply only to the living. However, Jefferson did not write that "all *living* men are created equal." From the perspective of a theory of humankind as an open society, extending indefinitely both into the past and into the future, let us attempt to unpack the ultimate meaning of Jefferson's words.

Not to take seriously the symbolic legacy of human beings wherever and whenever it is discovered amounts both to disenfranchising the excluded human beings from the open society and to impoverishing one's own culture. However, such acts of disenfranchisement and impoverishment occur regularly in the presently reigning theories of democracy. The symbols of the ancient myths, of Greek philosophy, of Israelite and Christian revelation, and of medieval mysticism tend to vanish into a memory hole in both secular liberal and radical theories of democracy. One has only to cite the notorious example of Karl Popper's *The Open Society and Its Enemies* to illustrate the tortured, diminished legacy left by the "Enlighteners." Indeed, for Popper almost all of the past, save for a ray of light here and there, is not only pre-democratic but even anti-democratic. How can this be, given that "all men are created equal"? Can our post-Enlightenment present be of so privileged a status as to render everything before the eighteenth century (or seventeenth or sixteenth) a history of crime and error?

Of course, it is possible to object that pre-"Enlightened" man was exploited and manipulated by the practitioners of witchcraft and "priestcraft," and that, accordingly, the rituals, myths and symbolisms of "early" (pre-modern) man were foisted upon an unsuspecting majority and did not represent their truly democratic wishes. (Indeed, Thomas Jefferson, who coined the term "priestcraft," was affected by this opinion of the Enlightened age of which he was a part.)

To reduce the greater part of human history to a story of a tiny minority of manipulators who pulled the strings of a vast majority of puppets is to strain credulity. One might immediately ask the question, "Where are the puppet-masters pulling the strings of today's puppets, who now say that all history can be written in terms of manipulators and manipulated?" And so one could continue in infinite regress. And one would have to ask, "What *deus ex machina* intervened at what point in history to unmask the manipulator's designs?" If one replied to the effect that modern "enlightenment" was the result of a steady biological evolution of the species, one would then be left with a theory that pre-eighteenth-century man was less than human, a theory which would strain the credulity of even the most ardent modernizer. For these and other reasons, I am not disposed seriously to pursue the manipulators vs. the manipulated thesis. Such a renunciation does not imply that I deny the existence of manipulators in history. Every age has had its Constantine, but without a climate of opinion already there his manipulations would come to naught. Furthermore, it is debatable whether Constantine manipulated the church or the church Constantine. Hardly a week goes by in one's personal life that does not attest both to the ubiquity and the ultimate irrelevance of "manipulativeness."

Looking back over the history of mankind as an open society, one can discover truths about the human condition in the ancient myths of the cosmos needed today to correct certain imbalances in the modern consciousness. The ecological movement is in many ways a fumbling attempt to rediscover the truth of the myth to the effect that man is a part of nature relating to it from within rather than subjugating it from without. Plato used the symbol *metaxy* (between) to indicate the character of political reality as a field of spiritual forces; to live as a human being means to exist in tension between the poles of life and death, good and evil, reason and appetite, the divine and the demonic, and so on.

The modern experiment desperately needs the wisdom of the Hebrew prophet Jeremiah, who reported the Lord of all flesh as condemning those who "seek great things for themselves." It is in Genesis (in a passage strangely ignored by Bergson) that man is presented as the creature made "in the image of God." The Christian doctrine of the Trinity affirms the threefold truth of God's absolute transcendence (God the Father), his self-sacrificial assumption of human form (God the Son), and his presence in the consciousness of universal mankind (God the Holy Ghost). The great mystics continually recalled the faithful from their tendency to substitute doctrine for experience by emphasizing that no propositional language is adequate to express the reality of divine presence. Philosophy can reason by analogy from what is capable of being experienced in an immanent fashion to what can only be grasped by the uncertain knowledge of faith; *viz.*, the Ineffable, the Unsayable.

From the perspective of the open society, modernity appears as a deeply troubled experiment that seems destined to fail. Perhaps a theory of democracy for the post-modern age will recognize that the disappearance of the gods of myth from the cosmos left the bond of faith as the only thread connecting the man of the world empty of gods with the Hidden God of philosophy and revelation. As Eric Voegelin has shown, this thread of faith, this uncertain knowledge of truth, may snap easily, and human beings can fall prey to "gnostic" movements promising a phony terrestrial salvation.

One alternative to the gnostic movements of political messianism has been a secular liberalism which proclaims the "autonomy" of politics and the irrelevance of spiritual concerns. Such a liberalism rests on a dogmatic closure to the evidence of man as the creature capable of experiencing the sacred dimension. A post-modern theory of democracy that recognizes universal mankind as an open society can avoid both the dogmatism of the Enlighteners and the fanaticism of the gnostics. It will be a democracy leavened by the faith of uncertain truth, in the sense of Hebrews 11: 1-3.

Henri Bergson made a decisive advance for democratic theory by tracing its roots to the open morality of the Gospels. As he put it:

> Humanity had to wait till Christianity for the idea of universal brotherhood, with its implication of equality of rights and the sanctity of the person, to become operative. Some may say that it has been a rather slow process. . . . It began, nevertheless, with the teachings of the Gospels, and was destined to go on indefinitely; it is one thing for an idea merely to be propounded by sages. . . ; it is very different when the idea is to broadcast to the ends of the earth in a message overflowing with love, evoking love in return. Indeed, there was no question here of a definitive body of wisdom, capable of being completely expressed in maxims. There was rather an indication of a direction, a suggestion of a method; at the most, a designation of an

end that would be only provisional, calling forth a perpetual renewal of effort. Such effort was bound to be, in certain individuals at least, an effort of creation. The method consisted in supposing possible what is actually impossible in a given society, in imagining what would be its effect on the soul of society, and then inducing some such psychic condition by propaganda and by example: the effect, once obtained, would retrospectively complete its course; new feelings, evanescent indeed, would call forth the new legislation seemingly indispensable to their appearance, and which would serve to consolidate them.[8]

Bergson's thesis that the roots of the modern democratic experiment are in the Gospels is a welcome antidote to the parochialism of modern secularist theories. However, it is not only the Gospels which proclaim "the idea of universal brotherhood, with its implication of equality of rights and the sanctity of the person." The Hebrew scriptures do so with equal profundity. Israel was the Chosen People only in the sense of carrying the weight of the obligation to serve the one, universal God. Israel is free of the confusion between "ecumenicity" and "universality."[9] Israel's mission was to serve as an example to the *goyim*. In no sense was Israel meant to engage upon an imperialistic crusade.

The basic flaw of Bergson's theory of democracy is its modernistic bias. He fails to remedy the Enlightenment's disenfranchisement of those people in the past whose cultures were centered on the compact myth of the cosmos. He only extends the enfranchisement back in time to the environment of the historical Jesus. What happens, however, to the universal Christ, the Christ of "Before Abraham was, I am," the Christ of Thomas Aquinas, who is acknowledged Head of all mankind from its unknown origin to its unknown end?

One does not have to accept the hierarchical division of caste and class reflected in the assumptions about social structure in the ancient myths to acknowledge the universal truth that those myths contained about the human condition. A valid democratic theory of today must be open to the contribution of the myth of the cosmos to our understanding of human sensibilities and to an enlargement of our symbolic horizon. Such a theory must also be open to theophanies wherever they occur, meaning that the great non-Western mystical and mythical symbolisms should not be rejected as in principle inferior because they are non-Western. Instead of the Westernization of the world through some neo-Napoleonic plan, we in the West should look forward to having our own world enriched by the awareness of different styles and models of the good life. Through the free play with symbols from Altamira on-wards, we in the modern West may become aware of the oneness of humankind, as it manifests itself in a multitude of equivalent symbolisms. Recovering the symbolic (as opposed to the literal) dimension and linking a valid theory of democracy to awareness of universal mankind as an open society are the two prerequisites for a fully developed democratic theory. As Bergson suggests, the open society idea, although not capable of propositional expression in maxims, would, to the degree that it was accepted, "call forth the new legislation seemingly indispensable" to it.

What is vital is always to keep in mind the following stipulation of W.H. Auden:

> When we use the word democracy we do not mean or should not mean any political constitution or political structure. All such matters are secondary. What we mean or ought to mean is the completely open society.[10]

Particular political structures, whether "pluralistic" or "participatory," are not and cannot be the equivalent of an open society. As I have suggested elsewhere, the best one can hope for in a given nation is that it be a society opening out to the true, the ultimate democracy: universal humankind, extending from its unknown origins to its unknown end. For such a nation, I have suggested the term "opening society."[11]

Notes

[1] C.B. Macpherson, "Pluralism, Individualism, and Participation," in *Economic and Industrial Democracy* I (London: SAGE, 1980), p. 24.

[2] Macpherson, "Needs and Wants: An Ontological or Historical Problem?" in Ross Fitzgerald, ed., *Human Needs and Politics* (London: Pergamon,

1977), p. 34. Emphasis in the original. I appreciate Mr. Macpherson's bringing these two essays to my attention.

[3] Dante Germino, "Henri Bergson: Activist Mysticism and the Open Society," *Political Science Reviewer* VII (1978): 3-40.

[4] Henri Bergson, *Two Sources of Morality and Religion*, trans. R. Ashley Audra and Cloudesley Brereton (New York: Henry Holt and Company, 1935), pp. 270-271. I have changed the translation of the fourth word of the quotation. The translators render *les conceptions politiques* "political systems." See Bergson, *Oeuvres* (Paris: Presses Universitaires de France, 1970), p. 1214.

[5] In 1967 Robert Dahl wrote that the "fundamental axiom" of American pluralism was that there be "multiple centers of power." Not even the people was sovereign. Public policy is formed through "peaceful negotiations between centers of power."

[6] See Dante Germino, *Political Philosophy and the Open Society* (Baton Rouge, La.: Louisiana State University Press, 1982), pp. 150-158 for a discussion of Bergson's distinction between the closed and the open morality.

[7] Raghuveer Singh, "Causality, Meaning and Purpose in Politics," Presidential Address to the Indian Political Science Conference, December 1978, p. 2.

[8] Bergson, *Two Sources*, pp. 70-71. I have revised the translation in places. See Bergson, *Oeuvres*, pp. 1040-41 for the original text.

[9] See Germino, *Political Philosophy and the Open Society*, pp. 96-104 for a discussion of the distinction between universal and ecumenic mankind, developed by Eric Voegelin. Briefly, ecumenic mankind is global humankind, gathering together all currently living human beings under one tent. Ecumenic mankind is an object of conquest by an Alexander or a Napoleon. Universal mankind has no time boundaries and it is not an object of conquest. It is humankind from its unknown origin to its unknown end.

[10] W.H. Auden, Commencement Address, Smith College, June, 1940.

[11] See Germino, *op. cit.*, pp. 182-183.

The Lure and
The Limits of Openness

R. Bruce Douglass

The open society in its more familiar sense, i.e. in Popper's sense, merits our close attention because it highlights fundamental problems and concerns endemic to modern nation states, particularly constitutional democracies.[1] There has been, of course, a quite different way of interpreting the meaning of openness in recent social and political theory, one associated with such figures as Henri Bergson and Eric Voegelin, and I mean no disrespect in neglecting their work here. As a matter of fact, the theories of openness which they have developed raise issues which are of the greatest philosophical and practical importance.[2] But their usage is idiosyncratic. It does not conform to the image of openness which most people have in their minds; and it does not have, in turn, much to do with the role that the idea of the open society has come to play as a cultural and political force in societies like the United States.

There is also, of course, an elaborate theory involved in Popper's usage, and I do not mean to suggest that this theory in its entirety has been absorbed into the public consciousness, much less that it has been widely accepted. Popper's theory is, in its own way, every bit as esoteric as those of Bergson and Voegelin. What I do mean to suggest, however, is that insofar as the idea of the open society conveys a meaning which is at all clear and comprehensible in popular and semi-popular usage – as I believe it does – that meaning is, for the most part, what Popper had in mind. The concept of openness is employed as a means of identifying the distinctive attributes of the social and political order of the Western democracies, and this is understood in a manner that reflects the characteristic biases and assumptions of Western liberalism.[3] Openness is associated primarily with freedom, and freedom is interpreted in the liberal manner. An open society is a free society, which means that it allows for the largely uninhibited pursuit of diverse (and competing) beliefs and practices. More is involved, however, than just the toleration of such diversity. Openness in Popper's sense suggests, above all, a society that makes such freedom – and the social and cultural pluralism that typically accompanies it – into a, or perhaps even *the*, primary virtue of social institutions. An open society treats individual freedom of thought and action as the highest good in the way that other societies dedicate themselves to the pursuit of virtue, justice, piety, etc. The concept derives its meaning and utility, in turn, from contrasting societies which actively pursue this end through a policy of laissez-faire, and those which have some other purpose and pursue it in a way that requires adherence to some sort of orthodoxy.

This idea obviously has considerable appeal, especially in the West. Exactly how much is not easy to say, but the very fact that it can be taken seriously as a characterization of the essential identity of the constitutional democracies speaks for itself. It represents a current of thought which is increasingly important to the way Western peoples conceive of the nature and purpose of their common life, and it finds growing expression in political practice. Despite this popularity, however, it has not achieved the standing to which its proponents, beginning with Popper, have aspired. At least not yet. Its influence falls well short of dominance, and it has not really succeeded in discrediting the alternative ways of conceiving social and political order it was meant to supplant. Instead, it is forced to co-exist, uneasily, with other competing currents that often contradict its most fundamental claims. Furthermore, the harder its proponents press their case – as in the current battles over the so-called "lifestyle" issues – the more they tend to generate active opposition.

Western consciousness is thus divided and ambivalent – deeply, if I read the signs correctly – about the issue Popper's theory raises.

The lure of openness is real, and it exerts a powerful pull. But so, too, does the notion of standing affirmatively for certain specific beliefs and practices; and to the extent that the former is in tension, if not contradiction, with the latter, the limits of its appeal quickly become evident. Especially as it becomes apparent that openness consistently applied could well be subversive of important features of the way of life to which Western peoples are accustomed do misgivings and even hostility begin to arise. This ambivalence is our main concern here. It is a phenomenon of considerable importance, and it deserves serious attention not only for what it reveals about Popper's theory but also, more broadly, for what it portends about the direction in which our civilization is moving as well. In speaking thus, however, I presuppose a particular way of interpreting it, one which requires explanation. I shall seek, on the one hand, to provide an explanation of its causes, and on the other, to offer a prediction as to its likely fate. In the process I hope to clarify the real logic of Popper's ideal and its place in the events of our time.

My central theme is the relationship between openness and modernization. Openness in Popper's sense is, I submit, largely a modern phenomenon, and the appeal it exercises today is best understood as a function of modernization. The ideal he presents is in fact just another name for a set of beliefs and values that have been an important part of modern thinking ever since the time of the Enlightenment. By this I do not mean that they are unique to the modern period. There are obvious antecedents which, as Popper shows, predate by many centuries the coming of modernity. But they are just that – antecedents; and contrary to the impression which Popper tries to create, the ideals which prevailed in pre-Platonic Athens are not in fact identical to openness as he conceives it. His ideal reflects a characteristically modern outlook that, predictably, is at best only partially approximated in the democratic thought of Greek antiquity; and the very different reception it has experienced in our time is a consequence, in turn, of the fact that the societies in question are ones in which the process of modernization is relatively far advanced.

It is my thesis, in turn, that modernization typically results in a set of social and cultural circumstances in which the qualities of mind and behavior that Popper associates with openness arise naturally and, in fact, are virtually indispensable. Given the conditions of life which a person growing up in a modern society confronts, it is hard to imagine escaping these qualities, to some extent at least, and they find reflection, in turn, in social institutions and policy. The role which they play is so important that they should be expected to have a strong appeal wherever modernization occurs; and the more modern a society becomes, the stronger should be the expected appeal – up to a point. The really interesting question, in turn, is why there is any resistance at all to their progress – as there obviously is today in societies where modernization is well advanced. Why does this occur – and on a scale that can hardly be dismissed as inconsequential? One possible answer is that modernization simply has not advanced far enough, and that the signs of resistance we currently see are just the vestiges of a pre-modern mentality that can be expected to fade with the passing of time. This is obviously what the proponents of Popper's way of thinking would have us believe, and part of it is indisputable. The resistance undeniably does reflect a reaction against some of what modernization brings, which grows out of an attachment to established beliefs and practices. It is a mistake, however, to attribute this simply to a traditionalist mentality that will dissolve as modernization advances. For it is not confined to those groups which are least modernized, but is spread widely across the population; and it seems, if anything, to be growing. The strongest support for Popper's ideal comes, to be sure, from the modernizing avant-garde, but the resistance is hardly confined to those who seek to be consistently anti-modern. Another explanation is in order, therefore, and I propose that it is to be found in what some observers have aptly characterized as the "discontents" of modernity – and the resulting impulses for "demodernization."[4]

Modernity is a condition which brings certain obvious and highly important benefits to those who experience it. But it also brings costs – psychic ones, especially – which are in their own way every bit as important. And a – I do not say "the" – natural response to these costs is to resist by trying to restrict the scope of modernization. Those who inhabit modern societies want, predictably, to have, as much as possible, the benefits without the costs; and they seek, therefore, to draw the line at some point in the process to prevent their being overwhelmed by the changes that it brings. It is just this sort of "drawing the line" which is at work in the negative reaction which many policy proposals reflecting Popper's ideal currently elicit. For even though they find appealing some of Popper's openness, large numbers of people in societies like the United States resist embracing it unequivocally. They resist accepting all that it implies, as the idea of a whole social and political order founded on the idea of openness would suggest. They resist it particularly in matters that are of great practical significance in their own lives – e.g., family law or policies concerning the education of the young – and threaten institutions to which they are deeply attached. The sources of this resistance are more basic than just cultural lag: they reflect a desire to maintain some sense of security, order and meaning in an environment where change is increasingly the norm. Above all, they reflect the desire to preserve and uphold a certain way of life which can only be effectively maintained *in common*.

Those who analyze modern societies in these terms are inclined, in turn, to argue that such feelings are endemic to modernity, and that, far from receding, they are likely to intensify in the foreseeable future. The more the effects of modernization are felt, the less can be taken for granted. Beliefs and practices inherited from the past will become increasingly precarious, and as the awareness of this develops, it is almost certain to evoke an increasingly powerful response. The latter part of this essay will explore the implications of this for the fate of Popper's ideal.

In attributing the appeal of the idea of openness to modern societies, I mean to invoke the familiar sociological distinction between modern and traditional societies.[5] The distinction is, of course, ideal typical. Nowhere is it fully realized in the world as we encounter it; actual societies always have a mixture of "modern" and "traditional" elements. But it is valuable, nonetheless, for it illuminates a difference that is of fundamental importance in making sense of a change in the way life is experienced in societies that have undergone successful modernization. Two aspects of that change are of particular importance here: one is the movement from fate to choice, and the other is a shift from parochial to cosmopolitan socialization. The significance which these factors have in the lives of modern people and the interplay between them is the source of the appeal that the idea of openness has come to exercise.

When compared with the consciousness which emerges as a result of modernization, nothing is more fundamental to the ex-

perience of pre-modern men and women than the sense that the
conditions of life are given, unalterable, and therefore simply to be
accepted, in much the same manner as the weather. To some extent, of course, *all* human beings, even the most modern, have to
accommodate their lives to certain givens. Even the most
dedicated proponent of the modern idea of progress must come to
terms with the unavoidable fact of his or her own finitude. But
there is an enormous difference between accommodating oneself to
some circumstances that are beyond control, and experiencing virtually all of one's existence in this way. There is, moreover, a most
important difference between a frame of mind which assumes the
desirability of reducing the role of fate in human existence as much
as possible and one which accepts its dominion as inevitable.

The striking thing about traditional societies, in turn, is how
readily the determination of a person's fate by forces beyond his
control is taken for granted as inevitable – and right. In such a
society almost every aspect of a person's existence, from how he
earns his livelihood to the composition of his diet, is experienced as
given, and there is little or no sense of the possibility of real
change. Life is what it has always been, generation after generation, and it is to be endured, not changed. Above all this is true of
one's place in the social order, which is experienced as having an
objectivity and permanence akin to that of the physical environment. Just as the sun rises daily in the east, so that one can
organize one's life on the premise that it will indeed appear there at
a certain time and not elsewhere, so, too, is it taken for granted
that the son of a peasant will also be a peasant, and live essentially
the same sort of life as his forebears. For him to do otherwise – e.g.,
to aspire to be a lord – would violate the natural order. Similarly,
for a woman to aspire to a role different from that traditionally
ascribed to her gender, or to seek even to order her household in a
manner significantly different from that sanctioned by tradition,
would be unthinkable. It is not only that such action would meet
with the disapproval of one's family and acquaintances. More fundamentally, to inhabit a pre-modern society – and to partake of pre-
modern consciousness – means that the very notion that life could
be changed into something significantly different is not likely to
arise. The whole weight of socialization is placed behind the in-
evitability of the existing order, so that the possibility of
choice – especially *individual* choice – does not even enter into

one's thinking.

Modernization, in turn, entails the decomposition of this objectivity and the creation of conditions in which individual choice is not only possible, but in fact increasingly difficult to avoid. This is hardly the place to enter into a detailed discussion of the process by which this occurs. But everywhere that it has happened, the emergence of a modern industrial sector, based on inanimate sources of energy, has been of fundamental importance. From the time of the Industrial Revolution, industrialization has produced what is justly characterized as a transformation of consciousness. The peasant who otherwise would have taken for granted that his destiny is to perpetuate the way of life passed down from his forebears encounters a new and altogether different world the moment he comes into contact with modern industry; and the more such a person is drawn into that world, the more his experience of life is bound to change. The mere existence of modern industry creates for such an individual the possibility of choice as never before, and participation in that world fosters an attitude toward change – in the first instance, technical change – that is altogether different from the mentality characteristic of traditional societies. And as the industrial sector grows, the opportunity for choice steadily expands. Especially as productivity increases and the division of labor is refined in accordance with the evolving demands of modern industry, the work that a person does is increasingly open to choice; and with vocational mobility other aspects of life begin to become matters of choice as well. Indeed, with the increases of education and material well-being which successful industrialization brings, one after another, many of the more important features of human existence come to be – potentially at least – matters of choice.

Grasping the opportunity to innovate this presents does not come automatically, of course. The unavoidable significance of the legacy which any new generation receives from its predecessors makes it probable that the outcome of the choices that are made will be a continuation, in some respects at least, of what has gone before. The first generation of industrial workers can be expected to behave in ways which reflect the persistence of beliefs and values that derive from the pre-industrial past of their families. But the more modern a society becomes, the less this can be taken for granted. For the presumption, increasingly, is that individuals have a right and even a *duty* to decide for themselves what to make of their lives; and as this develops into a conscious ethic, it is almost certain to lead to individual choices which profoundly alter the character of the social order. Translated into the notion of equality of opportunity as it is commonly interpreted today, for example, it carries the implication that an individual should *not* in fact be content with the situation in life of his parents, but instead should strive for social mobility. The same child who assumes the right to elect a vocation different from that of his parents also comes to take for granted, moreover, that the design of his "personal" life is also a matter that should be decided primarily, if not exclusively, on the basis of personal taste. So whether or not he will marry, to whom, for how long, under what conditions, etc., is all open to decision, which entails the the very real possibility that the character of personal life may change profoundly from one generation to the next.

As part of this process, the same attitude comes to prevail with respect to one's *Weltanschauung*, or worldview, as well. This is manifested most obviously in the change which takes place with respect to the status of religious beliefs and practices. Whereas once it was taken for granted that the members of a particular society would share in common a certain religious identity and any private reservations they might have about the details of orthodoxy would be suppressed, in a modern society religion increasingly becomes a matter of "preference," and even those who identify with a particular religious tradition reserve the right to define the meaning of that identification for themselves. Inevitably there are, again, important changes in the transition from one generation to another. The family which for generations has taken for granted a certain faith as part of its very identity suddenly confronts the prospect of one or more of its members adopting, perhaps because of intermarriage, a different religious identity; or alternatively, it confronts a refusal to "opt" for any religious tradition whatsoever.

Increasingly, therefore, life is experienced as a series of choices that have to be made, with less and less taken for granted. This begins at a very early age, with the child being asked to think for himself ("What do you want to be when you grow up?"), and it continues for a long time. If current fashions in the industrially advanced societies are any indication of what is to come, the tendency will be to press the boundaries of choice further and further, so that to the end life will be experienced as an unending series of choices. Thus, as technology continues to advance and we move into the so-called "post-industrial" era, one will have the opportunity to choose not just one career, mate, family, etc., but several, and all the way along there will be encouragement, if not even pressure, to reconsider the choices made to date.

To the extent, in turn, that such opportunity for choice is valued and cultivated, it almost inevitably leads to increasing social and cultural pluralism.[6] Such a positive response is not to be taken for granted, to be sure. There are reasons, as we shall see, why a society might react negatively to the consequences of such expanding freedom of choice and seek to limit its range. But in the absence of such constraints it can be expected to produce steadily increasing variety in the beliefs and practices which members of the same society adopt. The society whose religious life has been dominated by one or two religious traditions, for example, is likely to find itself vulnerable to the proliferation of a series of new and different sects. In like manner, the imposition of a preferred way of living based on certain very definite values can be expected to give way increasingly to a variety of "lifestyles," which not only reflect different and even opposed values but are treated as "options" to be experimented with as life unfolds.

The encounter with diversity to which such pluralism leads is one of the most important parts of being modern, and it above all else is the reason why the idea of openness has the appeal that it does. For with such pluralism inevitably arises a problem that is potentially very troublesome, and is in principle of such great significance that it may be considered one of the great challenges of social policy of our time. Any society that encourages and indeed embraces freedom of personal choice in the way that modern societies tend to is almost certain to give rise to a variety of different subcultures, some of whose beliefs and practices are in serious conflict; and the obvious problem is how, in the light of such conflict, they can be integrated into a stable, harmonious whole. If social order is to be maintained and important social goods are to be achieved, a way must be found to enable these different communities to relate peacefully to one another and even to cooperate in the pursuit of common goods. What better answer to this problem, in turn, than the policy of social and cultural laissez-faire suggested by Popper? "You go your way, and I shall go mine, but each of us will respect the right of the other to think and act as he or she chooses. . . ." The more an individual or an institution has to deal directly with the reality of the sort of pluralism that entails any significant conflict of beliefs and values, the more the logic of such a policy quickly becomes apparent; and the more this experience is repeated, the more its appeal is likely to grow. The more families with established religious identities have to confront directly the reality of religious pluralism through intermarriage, for example, the more people are likely to be drawn to some sort of ecumenical toleration as the only practical way to deal constructively with the practical problems posed by the competing demands of the different faiths. Similarly, the more school systems have to confront the reality of cultural pluralism, the more educational policy is likely to reflect a policy of either neutrality or least common denominator on any issue (e.g. abortion) involving conflicts in beliefs or values among important subcultures.

It is characteristic of modern societies, in turn, for the opportunities for such experiences to multiply steadily. As industrial technology reshapes the social landscape, subcultures that previously lived in relative isolation from one another find it increasingly difficult to do so. They are drawn closer and closer into involvement with one another in a variety of different ways. There tends, for example, to be an enormous increase in geographic mobility deriving from the availability of modern means of transportation and the career mobilities that go with an industrial economy. The family that once considered rootage in a certain locale to be part of its identity suddenly finds some of its members moving to new places in search of work, where quite different beliefs and values may prevail; and the more modern a society becomes, the more frequent such moves are likely to be. As industrial societies mature, in fact, it is not at all uncommon for a person to relocate several different times, perhaps abroad as well as within his or her own nation, in the course of a lifetime. The social experience of those who find themselves moving from one place to another in this way is almost certain to be different from those who do not leave "home," and the more the movement, the greater the difference is likely to be. The Protestant who has never known a Jew may well find himself with a Jew for a college roommate, and may well settle later in a neighborhood where he rubs shoulders regularly with Catholics, secularists, etc.; and in the process of interacting with such people he is almost certain to become a different person. The particular communities to which such people move are also affected. They tend to become more pluralistic, and in the process lose much of their distinctiveness. The Californian who settles in Alabama is likely to embrace a different set of values than those which have traditionally prevailed in the American South, and the more such "outsiders" enter into the life of Southern communities, the more those other values can be expected to play a role in shaping the character of these communities.

Even those who never leave home, therefore, are likely to be affected, for the native population in one community after another inevitably has to deal with the effects of this migration to and from the wider society (and, indeed, the world). The good Swiss burgher who has no intention of ever leaving his beloved Lausanne has to deal with a foreign presence in his community that increasingly affects in a very serious way the quality of life and the character of public policy. As the demographics change, many other things tend to change as well, from sexual mores to the design of education. It is not just population mobility, moreover, which has this effect. New technological and commercial forces impose themselves ever more forcefully from outside with the coming of an advanced industrial economy. The most obvious of these forces are, of course, radio and television, but hardly less important is the transformation which retail trade undergoes as a result of the rise of firms which have a national and even international character. Both have essentially the same effect: they break down the walls of particularity which before their advent made it possible for life in one community to be significantly different from that in another. Just as radio and television have the effect of homogenizing the news and entertainment to which people are exposed, so, too, chain retailing homogenizes the goods that we buy and indeed the very tastes that we bring to the marketplace.

Increasingly, therefore, people feel themselves to be – whether they like it or not – part of a cosmopolitan society, in which it is virtually impossible to avoid extensive contact with men and women whose beliefs and practices differ significantly from one's own. The only way to do so effectively is to isolate oneself, like the Amish, from the whole culture. Barring that, the contact is bound to occur – and in forms that are not at all inconsequential. If it does not take place in one's own family, it occurs at work; and if it does not happen there, in the neighborhood; and if not there, in the television programs and commercials that one watches; and so on. The more the forces which make for modernization have their effect, moreover, the more likely it is that such encounters will not be episodic, but constant; and as this occurs, accommodation to pluralism will tend to become a constraint on thought and behavior that is simply taken for granted.

In suggesting that openness in Popper's sense exercises a natural appeal in the context of modern societies, I do not mean to imply that adjustment to the way of thinking it represents comes easily or that, in the last analysis, it provides a satisfactory solution to the problem which is the source of that appeal. There is, to be sure, a frame of mind which develops in modern societies which is (or at least appears to be) fully at home with the sort of "live and let live" ethic that the idea of openness entails, and the further the process of modernization advances, the more popular that mentality tends to become. For people who come to think in this way, toleration tends to be not just a practical necessity but a matter of principle as well. They, like Popper, view it as the *right* way to live—indeed, as the foundation of the good society. Before such a frame of mind is achieved, however, there typically is a history of painful adjustments to the reality of pluralism. The pain may or may not be a part of the lived experience of those who embrace the openness ethic; frequently the psychic costs are imposed mainly on the preceding generation. But somewhere those costs are felt, and they take a definite toll.

For what is involved in accommodation to pluralism is acceptance of the legitimacy of beliefs and values that are different and in some cases contrary to one's own. More to the point, it involves accepting institutions and policies in which such alien beliefs and values find expression. For any dedicated believer this can hardly be altogether satisfying. For it means the breaking down of traditions which embody cherished beliefs and values and the creation of an environment in which those beliefs and values may well find it very difficult to endure. The apologist for openness typically denies, of course, that any such threat exists, arguing that different traditions can co-exist with no adverse effect on their vitality, and indeed that they are likely to be enriched by interaction with one another. But the devout parent who confronts the prospect of the intermarriage of one of his children knows intuitively that the matter is not nearly so simple as such clichés would suggest. If he thinks at all realistically about what is involved in the mixing of different religious traditions in one household, he knows that it will in fact be very difficult to bring them together in a way that does not significantly dilute the vitality of one or both. Above all, parents in such a situation will worry that the household which results from such a marriage is likely to be a very uncertain conveyor of the beliefs and values they cherish to the next generation. Similarly, a homogenous community with a well-established cultural identity may take pride in the new wealth or "progress" which comes with the introduction of new industry but at the same time worry about the social consequences of the new and different kinds of people who accompany it. The natives sense, correctly, that the more the community is subjected to the influence of people from outside, the more difficult it will be to preserve the old ways, and there is no guarantee that what endures will be that which is really worth preserving.

The further modernization proceeds, moreover, the more obvious it becomes that such fears are justified. Intermarriage *does* tend to dilute the vitality of religious practice, if not belief, and mixed marriages do, typically, turn out to be less reliable instruments for the transmission of religious tradition. In like manner, the introduction of external forces embodying alternative beliefs and values *is* in fact very likely to subvert the way of life of an established community, and in ways which can easily do violence to cherished traditions. It is increasingly evident, as such effects accumulate, that more is involved than just the intermingling of existing subcultures. The magnitude of the changes modernization brings and the pattern to which they tend to conform suggest that modernization is itself a value-laden process which actively favors certain ways of thinking and being at the expense of others, and that most of what it promotes is inimical to the survival of traditional beliefs and values. Far from being neutral, therefore, as Popper's conception would suggest, the culture of modernity is in fact highly partisan, and what it promotes is more – much more – than simply the freedom to choose.

The freedom is there, to be sure, and it is undeniably an important part of what modernity entails. But at the same time it is only one part; if it is to be understood realistically, it needs to be seen in the context of the rest of modernization's fruits. The same process whereby the opportunities for personal choice multiply also brings into being a social order and a culture that actively predispose people to use these opportunities in a certain way. There are those who resist, of course, but the striking thing about modern societies, given the range of opportunities for choice available in principle, is how much homogeneity they tend to have, especially with regard to fundamental beliefs and values. Superficially there is, of course, extraordinary variety, but fundamentally there is an essential sameness about the way modern people think and act – which is surprising, in turn, only if one fails to take into account how much of what goes into the making of a modern society presupposes the secular, this-worldly, and above all materialistic outlook that has been characteristic of the "modernizers" ever since at least the seventeenth century.[7]

The promotion of this outlook tends to be accompanied by a progressive secularization of public life in which the status of alternative beliefs and values is rendered increasingly tenuous. In the name of tolerance, for example, moral teaching which derives from particular religious traditions is excluded from – or at least rendered anomalous in – public education and public law; and to the extent that moral values are bound up with religious and other beliefs that are peculiar to particular subcultures, the place of morality itself in public affairs is suspect (thus the tendency, perfectly exemplified by Popper, to make value relativism the effective basis of public life). In practice, of course, the results of such "neutrality" are not really neutral at all. Implicitly – and sometimes explicitly as well – certain beliefs and practices are actively promoted, but they are treated differently because they are not "sectarian." The whole ethos of public education in the United States has long promoted certain values which are of fundamental importance in character development – the autonomy of secular learning, for one, and conformity to majority norms, for another – but this is rarely viewed as anomalous because the values in question are supposedly shared by the society as a whole.

The more obvious this pattern becomes, in turn, the more likely it is to evoke a reaction. Those whose beliefs and values are threatened will be inclined to see the threat for what it is, and take steps to resist. At the least, they will demand a fairer opportunity for their views to endure and have influence. But one can easily imagine a more extreme reaction, so that the idea of what the open society represents is rejected in principle. Particularly if the challenge to traditional beliefs and practices is perceived to be so powerful and all pervasive that it allows no room for compromise, could those who feel themselves threatened be drawn to reassert the value of a specific orthodoxy; as this idea is pursued, it could well become a matter of principle. Once the suspicion dawns that the idea of openness is simply a Trojan horse for certain specific anti-traditional beliefs and values, it may in fact be difficult to avoid this conclusion.

Such a reaction, moreover, need not be confined simply to a small minority. To be sure, those whose beliefs and values are *consistently* anti-modern are not likely to comprise a large group in any society where modern conditions are at all well developed. But even in a society where modernization has proceeded very far, the number of people who are consistently modern in outlook and behavior is also not likely to be large. The vast majority will be drawn to *both* traditional and modern beliefs and values, and their lives will reflect compromises between the two, in various different forms. The engineer who in his daily work is a model of secular rationality may in his "private" life cling fiercely to certain practices that are un-mistakably pre-modern. Or those who inhabit – or even preside over – identifiably modern institutions may have in their minds, in spite of the "official" roles they play, certain pre-modern assumptions about how those institutions should operate (e.g., the corporation as "family"), and seek somehow to recreate the old ways. This could be interpreted, of course, in terms of cultural lag, so that it should be only a matter of time before such pre-modern beliefs and practices atrophy altogether. But an alternative explanation, which I think more accurately reflects the experiential basis of this phenomenon, is that in reality the beliefs and practices which are promoted by modernization are not always preferable to those which they would displace; the further modernization progresses, the more obvious this becomes. People cling to traditional beliefs and values, in certain aspects of their lives at least, precisely because they do not prefer the alternative which thorough modernization would bring.

The problem goes deeper, however, than simply the artificiality of the idea of the open society under the conditions which typically prevail in a modern society. Once this is recognized, it could be met, presumably, by efforts to apply Popper's idea more consistently.

Hypothetically, at least, one can imagine a society dedicating itself to reducing the influence of the implicit biases of modern culture so as to allow for greater real freedom of choice and variety. One can imagine a society restructuring its whole life, including everything from the education of the young to the conduct of economic activity, so as to insure the possibility of a wide variety of different subcultures co-existing side by side. Whether such an objective is in fact a practical possibility under modern conditions is, of course, anything but obvious, but let us assume for the moment that it is. The question, in turn, would be: If modern societies could somehow be reordered so as to make possible a truly equal opportunity to embrace any and all possible beliefs and values, including those which are not "progressive" as well as those which are, would openness in Popper's sense then constitute a worthy social ideal, one which would do justice to the aspirations and expectations that men and women today bring to the experience of living together in society?

Even under such ideal conditions, I would submit, Popper's vision would be unlikely to prove appealing, and the more its implications are spelled out, the more obvious the reasons become. One need only consider briefly the conditions that would have to be created in pursuit of such an ideal to see what costs it would impose. The most predictable consequence would be to reduce the scope of public policy to a minimum. In a society in which the goal is to avoid imposing any particular set of beliefs or practices as normative, there would be every reason to reduce the range of activity governed by public law as much as possible. The more laws that are passed and the more the scope of the law expands, the greater the likelihood of favoring certain beliefs and practices at the expense of others. The "positive" state is almost by definition a partisan in the struggle among competing subcultures, and so must be considered incompatible with Popper's ideal, to the extent it is consistently applied. Since the idea of openness exercises some of its strongest appeal among people who are also exponents of an activist role for government, this is a point which needs to be carefully underscored. Despite their common association, the two ideas are simply not compatible. The more consistently one tries to apply either of them, the more the other is sure to be a casualty.

More is involved here, however, than simply the fate of government activism as we have come to think of it since the creation of the welfare state. Not just the welfare functions of government would be eliminated, but all of those measures by which a certain way of life is promoted. In a society which seriously applies itself to pursuing Popper's ideal, all of those elements in the law which favor one way of life over another would have to be purged. To take an example that is particularly important and sensitive today, all of those laws and policies which favor the institution of heterosexual, monogamous marriage would be have to be rewritten so as to reflect an equal respect for alternative arrangements. The same would apply, of course, to family law. All of those features of existing legal systems which are designed to encourage and promote a certain pattern of family life would need to be eliminated. For in no sense would it be appropriate for the law to function as a tutor in relation to the way in which people choose to arrange this most private aspect of their lives.

The problem with this is obvious: it makes the individual freedom of choice into an absolute, and in the process strips the law of any possibility of performing what historically has been perhaps its most important function, the cultivation and protection of a certain way of life. Law in the past has hardly ever been the neutral instrument Popper's idea would imply, and the reason is an elementary sociological fact. To be "a people" is more than just to inhabit a certain territory. It is to share together a common way of being which, almost by definition, is based on certain rather definite values. The whole structure of a society, including all of its major institutions, typically reflects such values, and this is accepted because most members take for granted that the values in question are not just "preferences" (as the positivist characterization would imply) but are, in some sense, the *right* way to live.

Pursuing Popper's ideal involves abandoning this way of thinking altogether. It means forsaking any possibility of using public power to promote and maintain a certain way of life – aside, of course, from what is required by openness itself. Whether it is in fact possible for a coherent social and political order to be constituted on this basis is, of course, not at all to be taken for granted; but assuming that it is, the question of whether it is desirable is still unanswered. More to the point, there still remains the question of whether the purposes that are served by such a single-minded preoccupation with individual freedom and autonomy are of such importance as to justify the almost certain costs that would be imposed with respect to the preservation of the values embodied in established institutions. The answer that most people can be expected to give, as these costs become apparent, is predictable. When it is recognized that openness consistently applied means giving no preference whatsoever to an institution like heterosexual, monogamous marriage, or the family built on that foundation, and treating all of the alternatives with equal respect, openness will be dismissed out of hand; and the more it is identified with an attack on the privileged standing of such institutions, the more problematic its status is likely to become.

The drift of my argument should be apparent by now. Openness, in the sense of respect and even appreciation for diversity of beliefs and practices, is an idea which, up to a point, makes very good sense in the context of modern societies. It makes such good sense, in fact, as a response to the social and cultural pluralism which would appear to be the natural by-product of the conditions created by modernization that one has a difficult time envisioning how – short of systematic denial of freedom – it could be dispensed with. This is why it enjoys such widespread appeal. It meets a need which is increasingly important the more modern a society becomes. At the same time, however, it is not at all clear that it provides an adequate basis for an entire social theory, as the idea of an open *society* would suggest. For such an idea implies that openness is to be treated as the primary social good, or at least the essential condition of that which is considered to be the primary good. It entails making openness the foundation on which the entire structure of a society is to be constituted and the principal criterion by which the worth of social policy is ultimately to be determined. The obvious question, in turn, is whether it is really capable of bearing this burden. By this I mean not just that a theory can be constructed on this basis, which is plausible as a hypothetical possibility, but also that the results of acting on such a theory would actually satisfy, as a practical matter, the aspirations of the people who inhabit modern societies. By presenting his theory as an articulation of the operative ideal of the Western democracies, Popper seeks to convey the impression that the answer is self-evident; but if the argument presented here is at all valid, it is anything but. For what I have sought to show is that far from being the actual basis of the institutional structure of Western societies, the idea which Popper presents is in fact highly innovative, and to the extent that it is actually pursued, it is likely to produce major changes in the way these societies are ordered. It represents, indeed, a radical departure from what has been the actual character of these societies, and the more it is pursued, the more obvious this can be expected to become.

The nature of the change involved is such, moreover, that it can hardly be expected to elicit a groundswell of consistent popular support, at least not as the larger implications become evident. As long as the focus is simply on the enhancement of personal autonomy which the idea of the open society entails, it can be expected to have considerable appeal. The freedom to live and act as one chooses is, for reasons I have sought to identify, something which modern men and women are inclined to value greatly. As important as such autonomy is, however, it is by no means the only thing which they value; when it becomes evident that the consequence of such a single-minded preoccupation with individual autonomy is likely to be the subversion of important features of the way of life to which they are accustomed, even modern people can be expected to have second thoughts. These misgivings can be expected to multiply as the magnitude of the changes at stake begins to be recognized. The manifold changes that would be required to bring existing law and public policy into conformity with the ideal of moral and philosophical neutrality that Popper's theory entails are, in fact, so far removed from the actual values and aspirations that people today bring to the experience of living together in society that it is difficult to imagine such a proposal even being taken seriously, much less adopted, once the consequences are clear.

That it *is* taken seriously may be attributed primarily to the fact that the consequences have not yet had to be confronted – that and the lack of a clear understanding of the alternatives. Precisely because Western societies have not in fact been constructed in the manner Popper's idea of the open society would suggest, the costs of acting consistently in terms of such a principle have not really had to be addressed. Because they have been able to take for granted a well-established social order that predisposes their fellow citizens to think and act in certain predictable ways, the inhabitants of these societies have been in a position to have their cake and eat it, too. They have been able, that is, to affirm, often virtually without qualification, the value of individual autonomy and pluralism, while simultaneously assuming that certain beliefs and practices will in fact prevail. The further modernization has proceeded, however, and the more vigorously Popper's ideal has been asserted, the less can be taken for granted about how people will choose to think and act. As established institutions are challenged and begin to lose their taken-for-granted quality, the possibility of a real pluralism begins to arise, and with it, the necessity of choice.

Already the choice is beginning to be made in the debate over such issues as abortion and the role of values in education, and the response is predictable. Confronted with the possibility of actually creating a society which conforms to Popper's ideal, the majority do not in fact embrace it. To be sure, they do not spurn the values that openness represents completely. But neither are they inclined to give them unconditional priority. Instead they seek compromise, in which a balance is struck between the competing claims of freedom for individuals, on the one hand, and the desire to maintain and protect an established way of life, on the other. The sort of neutrality in law and public policy which Popper's idea of openness entails is accepted, and even affirmed, up to a point. Insofar as it is taken to mean simply ridding individuals of the burden of unwarranted and oppressive intrusion in their personal lives, it generally meets with approval. But when it is taken literally, so that law can in no sense reflect particular beliefs and values that might be objectionable in some quarter, it generally meets with active resistance. In fact, with very few exceptions, it tends consistently to be rejected.

This is usually done, to be sure, with some uneasiness. Because of the enormous value which Western peoples have come to place on personal autonomy, and because they themselves are anxious to preserve the liberties which their societies currently afford, most of those who resist embracing what Popper's ideal entails do so with hesitation. For in a setting so deeply influenced by the spirit of modern individualism, there tends almost always to be a presumption of illegitimacy connected with any policy that appears to diminish or compromise personal liberty. The proponents of Popper's ideal play on this, of course. They seek to portray any policy which fails to give to individual autonomy the primacy they advocate as an attack on freedom. Thus it is that almost any attempt to have public policy conform to particular beliefs and values, even those of a large and enduring majority, on a contested issue is liable to be stigmatized as oppressive. As long as the majority can be persuaded to believe this, they will be on the defensive. In particular, as long as they continue to think in terms of simplistic dichotomies such as "open" vs. "closed" societies will they have difficulty pursuing their interests effectively.

To some extent, such defensiveness is unavoidable. It is part of the ambivalence which has been my theme, and it is probably inherent in the experience of being modern. Modern people can be expected to have such conflicting feelings as long as they are modern. For the reasons I have sought to elaborate, however, there are grounds for believing that a new phase in the development of modern consciousness is in the making. Necessity is the mother of invention, and the time may well be approaching when the discontents of modernity will crystallize in a new way of thinking that entails a new appreciation of the value and importance of community. The late modern experiment with doctrinaire individualism may well be playing itself out; and to the extent that this occurs, the limits of Popper's ideal can be expected to become even more apparent than they already are. They may in fact render it obsolete; and the irony is that if this occurs, it will be precisely the radicalism of the individualism it represents which produces this result. Confronted with the real implications of the individualistic doctrines to which they have been attracted to date, modern people may finally begin to appreciate the costs they impose.

Notes

[1] The principal statement of the theory of the open society elaborated by Karl Popper is his *The Open Society and Its Enemies*, 2 vols. (London: Routledge and Kegan Paul, 1945). For a refinement of this position, see also his "On Reason and the Open Society," *Encounter* 38 (May, 1972): 13-19.

[2] I have discussed some of these issues elsewhere in "What Does It Mean to Be Open?," *Teaching Political Science: Politics in Perspective* 11 (Fall

1983): 21-28.

[3] For a discussion of Popper's theory as a variant of liberalism, see my "Liberalism as a Threat to Democracy" in F. Canavan, ed., *The Ethical Dimension of Political Life* (Durham: Duke University Press, 1983), 28-39.

[4] Cf. Peter Berger, Brigitte Berger, and Hansfried Kellner, *The Homeless Mind—Modernization and Consciousness* (New York: Random House, 1973).

[5] Berger, Berger and Kellner develop this distinction at some length. See also Marion Levy, Jr., *Modernization and the Structure of Societies* (Princeton: Princeton University Press, 1966) and C.E. Black, *The Dynamics of Modernization* (New York: Harper & Row, 1966).

[6] An obvious question that is bound to arise is how modernization relates to societies that develop under totalitarian regimes. These societies, especially in their communist form, aspire to modernity, yet they are hardly open in Popper's sense. I would propose that most of the phenomena to which I attribute the appeal of openness do in fact exist in such places, with much the same effects as in constitutional democracies. Even in these supposedly monolithic societies, there are strong pressures to enhance the individual's freedom of choice, and to the extent that these pressures have an effect, they are bound to increase the amount of social and cultural pluralism. Contrary to what some of the more simplistic clichés about totalitarianism suggest, moreover, some degree of this is entirely compatible with the logic of totalitarian rule. Stalin's brutal "revolution from above" in the 1930s, for example, even though it visited the worst sort of tyranny on millions, also created the conditions for unprecedented social mobility in Russia. Millions had their lives ruined at the point of a gun, but millions of others had opportunities opened up for them that they surely would scarcely have imagined otherwise. Totalitarian regimes generally have had, in fact, a strong modernizing thrust, and for this reason have been, in their own peculiar way, agents of emancipation for individuals. However, they are not at all consistent in this regard. They seek to liberate people from the "idiocy" of backwardness, as Marx would put it, and establish a social order appropriate for modern men and women. But they are unwilling to accept the differences of opinion which inevitably accompany the individualism modernization brings. They are unwilling, in fact, even to tolerate significant dissent. So they must impose conformity, and the effort required to maintain even an approximation of the degree of conformity they seek under modern conditions is enormous. As such societies mature, it becomes progressively harder to achieve this. The more successful they are at modernization, the more they tend to create a citizenry unfit for such domination. This is the underlying problem in domestic politics throughout the industrialized sector of the communist world, and it could ultimately prove to be the undoing of these regimes. As many of their more prescient

leaders seem to recognize, they face a stark choice: either they adapt to the new realities created by modernization or they will not be able to govern successfully.

[7] Modern science, for example, is built on the premise of metaphysical materialism, and the more influential it has become as a cultural force, the more it has tended to make materiality the measure of reality. That which is not material – " 'just' an idea" – is rendered increasingly unreal. Similarly, modern industry and commerce, which together have constituted such a powerful force in the reshaping of both the material and the social conditions of life in modern societies, have functioned like a magnet for the creative energies of modern men and women, drawing them increasingly into the domination and exploitation of the material world and inclining them to think of such activity as the primary human vocation. The success of this effort has been enormous, of course, with the result that modern societies (especially those with capitalist economies) have come to take for granted a level of wealth that is unprecedented and can be successfully absorbed only by actively cultivating human acquisitiveness on a mass scale. This naturally finds expression in modern culture which, especially since the advent of mass consumption, has almost invariably had a predominantly materialistic orientation.

Activity, Philosophy,
and the Open Society

Joseph Cropsey

The coiner of the expression "open society" is, of course, free to appropriate those words to the meaning that he has in mind in inventing the term; but when he uses that freedom, he stimulates us to wonder about the meaning of that combination of words in itself and apart from his intention. Here, I propose to look at the expression "open society" naively, as if to ask without partiality what an open society might be.

In what way or ways can a "society" be "open"? The question may be approached through openness itself: what are the ways of openness? A flower, a door, and an eye can be open, but each only in its own way. The flower, as open, is an entity that has undergone a change which we think of as a development, that is, an ascent, in the course of which a fullness that was potential and concealed came out into the open or into the light of day. Obedient to influences hard to define, the flower has disclosed either itself or those "influences" that are at work on itself and has arrived at an openness which is, by the way, the necessary prelude to its decline *out* of the light of day. For a society to be open in this sense, it must have reached a fulfillment implicit in its kind, either *qua* society or *qua* particular regime, or merely *qua* individual state; and that in turn means that societies, regimes and countries belong to the class of entities that unfold, stand forth in revelation, and then shut down towards death. History appears to confirm beyond doubt that political beings belong to that class. It seems, then, that an open society is one whose truest, most inward being has come to light in a concrete efflorescence, fated some day to dissolve.

Is it possible to say precisely and concretely what would stand forth revealed in the fullness of society's openness? Would one recognize that fullness in a moral fact? in a condition of high culture – music, literature, the arts? in a perfection of religious life? in a plenitude of wealth and power? or perhaps in a state of perfect concord among the inhabitants of the realm? In groping toward the indispensable concreteness, we find ourselves in need of an answer to the question, What is society? Thus, if it were true that the essence of society is a bondedness, a being drawn together, a likemindedness, mutuality or "integration" of members, then the fully opened society would be the society that is most nearly a One. When Aristotle criticizes the Platonic scheme of communism, he shows reasons for rejecting this conception of society, although when he insists that there be a friendship as well as a justice among men who form a polis, he seems to require that a society possess exactly such a bondedness if the members are to be free men rather than slaves. For the present purpose, it is sufficient to say that society is some kind of a one that has emerged from a many. The open society, then, is the one that has reached and disclosed the proper *concord* of unity, participation, and distribution that lies in the essence of society itself.

It is impossible to come to that conclusion without putting aside all the other suggested ends or goods of society – aesthetic, moral, imperial, religious, or still others. For example, it is conceivable that a society has opened to its fullness when human productivity has reached a peak within it: when its musical tradition has produced a Bach, its literature a Shakespeare, and its sculpture a Michelangelo; or rather, to follow another road, that its moral practice has reached the austerity of Geneva. How may the society be judged with regard to its openness if these various fulfillments are not synchronous, as in fact they need not be? Perhaps the problem can be solved only by ordering these regions of perfection, which means referring them all to the meaning of society itself and ranking them according to their proximity to that core of society's being. Even this will not do, because it implies that it is by virtue of the nature of society that, for example, unity stands highest, art next, and morality next in the order of fulfillments – that it is more important that a society be one than that it be artistic or moral, if it is to be considered open. The actual order of these criteria is irrelevant to my purpose, for I wish to maintain only that the conception of open society that assimilates opening to efflorescence eventually falls back upon some definition of essential society, society-in-itself, a thing that does not effloresce but without which the efflorescence of society is incomprehensible. To be as explicit as possible, the essence of society determines the openness of society not so much in that the essence is the definition of society but rather in that it is necessary for knowledge or recognition of the openness of society. Openness as efflorescence is derivative from essence: the concept of "open" *in this mode* is therefore not available to anyone who rejects the reality of an essence that stands in the background to vouchsafe a meaning to the word "open" so used in reference to society. The investigation of that essence is philosophy.

Even without claiming to be thorough, we saw at the outset that there are three apparently quite different modes of open: as a flower, as a door, and as an eye. While we say commonly that the door is open, we mean that the doorway is unobstructed and that the *house* is open. An open passage is a neutral access to some space that is receptive to being filled with what is outside yet capable of being inside. Our next task is to think about a society that is open in the way in which an open house is open. We know what an open house is open *to*: it is open to strangers, outsiders, anyone outside who prefers to be inside, and it is open to whatever is in the air. Eventually we will have to ask ourselves what class or classes of things are free to enter – or in principle to leave – the open society without hindrance. It is obvious that more is involved than the migration of people. I should like to put off the consideration of this point until later and to take up instead the question, What is the meaning of the condition of openness in a society? with a view especially to the related question, By what agency or means is the openness of a society brought about? The restriction of these questions to the mode of openness indicated by the figure of the house and its door is always to be understood. In terms of that image, I am asking something like, What is the state of a house with an open door, and how can one understand the coming to be of that openness?

An open house is one whose master does not have control over the relation between what stands without and what stands within. An open society, correspondingly, would resemble, to use another image, a living cell in which the osmotic process had gotten so far out of order that material passed arbitrarily in both directions through the cell wall. This would kill the cell, but I do not wish to say straightaway that the same condition would kill the society; I wish rather to think about the masterlessness of such a state or the utter passivity of it.

In order to understand the passivity of openness, we must grasp the determination of the society, just as we would have to conceive clearly the walls of the house or the cell, if we were to think profitably about the comings and goings between the thing and its externality. What determines or constitutes a society? (I should make clear that I have in mind society in its most intense form, namely, political society.) I will accept as well established the proposition that what constitutes the political society is its constitution. That being stipulated, the passivity of a political society, and therewith its openness in the present sense, would mean the uncontrolled movement of extraneous material into the body of the constitution, say by amendment or simply through usage, and the similar elimination of material from it through desuetude, interpretation, or in any other way.

The imputation of deliberate agency and therewith of active conscious choice, in this remark on constitutions in flux, will be weakened as soon as we make explicit that the constitution need not at all be written. Thus, amending the constitution might have very little in common with our own well-defined procession of steps for proposing and ratifying an amendment. Where the constitution is unwritten and the flux of the constitution is not governed by any identifiable agent's intention, the question arises immediately: Who is responsible for the change? And that question points to the larger one: Who or what is at the source of the constitution as a whole? These questions come into view through our interest in the openness of society as equivalent to the passivity of society. In order to defend the open society from the imputation of passivity, we are searching for an agent whose *active* choice determines the society, i.e., its constitution, and determines also the changes of the constitution. We are perhaps searching for the self of a political society. If we fail to find such a thing, we shall have to entertain the possibility that the open society is an object at the mercy of history, whatever that proves to mean. That, were it to eventuate, would be worth noting, if only for the reason that a famous advocate for the open society considers it to be rationalized exactly as the antithesis of historicism, of theories proclaiming a necessity in history that must stifle the freedom and reason of open society. But without an autonomous society-self determining the flux into and from the constitution of the society, the open society appears heteronomous, adrift, and passive – especially passive.

In order to avoid that conclusion if possible, let us boldly suppose that what we call metaphorically the society-self is non-metaphorically the likemindedness, concord, or consensus of all those who associate. Then this likemindedness is the active regulator of the egress and ingress between open society and its externality. But besides the dubiousness of personifying Concord and making of it an active being, a god of sorts, there is the vexing question of the *origin* of that likemindedness. In the first place, it might be attributed to something simply present in all the associators, something that they share and that makes them see the decisive political things in one and the same way. This breaks down as soon as we recognize that such an explanation is tanta-mount either to maintaining that there are innate, natural insights regarding constitutions – in which case, presumably, these would be shared by all men and there would be a single constitution for all of mankind – or that there are local concords of limited duration, generated by what we loosely call circumstances, such as the climate, the soil, the sea, the mines, and threats or opportunities of-fered by neighboring populations. In this latter case, the like-mindedness would be a simple product of the external circum-stances acting as causes to determine a group of minds in a single mold. Such a concord would be merely the indirect means by which the external circumstances would operate as remote causes of, in the present case, the adoption and alteration of constitutions. In no way, then, does anything we have yet uncovered point to the autonomous society-self whose activity would secure the open society against the imputation of passivity.

There is yet another path on which to seek the source or nature of the common mind of society, and that is the one indicated by the old notion that the laws and constitution are the educators of men. It is obvious immediately that the truth of this adage would seem to remove all support from the proposition that there is an *autonomous* social concord that regulates the gate through which migrations into and out of the constitution take place. We would be asserting that the constitution forms the men and the men so formed allow a free flow of alien material into the regime and of domestic material out of it; that is to say, they then form it *after* it has formed them. The circularity of the influence of regime on men and men on regime significantly weakens the argument for the existence of an autonomous and hence active agent in the open society as such; but we must be careful not to exaggerate the scope of that circularity. It would be such an exaggeration to deny, for example, that the open constitution might teach men that they are free to deform the constitution in any way they like. Astonishingly, the constitution might form its pupils to betray it by deforming it according to their own independent lights. Rather than that, it might admonish them, indeed form them in the belief, that the one thing they are not free to reject or modify is the openness of the regime. Such a restriction would not offend logic but it would certainly deprive the successive generations of men of their absolute freedom or autonomy as agents. Stated otherwise, it violates the premise of openness in the society, understanding openness as analogous to the removal of the door from its hinges at the entrance to the house with the concomitant freedom of *every* element of the constitution to depart the structure.

Perhaps the last word we need say on this part of the subject is at once the simplest and the most inclusive: the very notion of the *formation* of men by an instrument which they legislate only in the weak sense of consenting to it is on its face a derogation from the autonomy we are seeking. Until we find that autonomy, we have not found the self-activation that can save the open society (in the mode of the open house) from the imputation that it is passivity masquerading as freedom.

Mindful of the passivity that permeates the openness of the open society in the present mode, we return to the question posed earlier, namely, By what agency or means is the openness of a society brought about? Surely there is no reason to accept as truth the mere prejudice that a passive progeny must have been engendered by a passive progenitor, whatever that might mean: perhaps there is decisive activity at its begetting. Let us begin again by returning to our image of the house and noticing the simplest fact about it: it consists of, it *is*, four walls and a roof. By its nature or essence it is an enclosure. The door is an exception to the enclosing integrity of the wall. That it is an indispensable exception or breach without which the house could serve no practical purpose does not affect its being an exception or breach. To correspond with the (openable) house in its enclosing integrity there is the constituted society, whose constitution distinguishes the order of life lived within its space from all orders that lie outside. Men live within a social space that is determined, given its boundaries and thus its shape or form, by the constitution. The tautologous cast of this statement – the social space is formed or constituted by the constitution – might be excused if the remark draws us closer to the perception of the constitution, and therewith the political society, as, respectively, an artificial horizon and the territory encompassed within that horizon – to borrow a famous metaphor. If we are in fact asking who draws the horizon around the open society, we find ourselves asking who defines the world for those who live within that horizon and that society, for beyond the horizon there is nothing on earth, though an infinity aloft. I will assume for purposes of the argument the answer most favorable to the presuppositions of the open society, namely, that the horizon is inscribed not by a stylus activated by any mechanism, whether historical or natural, but by an active human agency that is free in the fullest sense possible. Without any attempt to defend this, I will suppose and assert that speculative reason is that consummately free human agency whose act and expression is philosophy. Granting this, if only to strengthen the case for autonomy and eventually authentic openness, we have arrived at the thought that it is philosophy that draws the horizons that constitute, define and bound or enclose the society whose possible openness is our problem.

Let us accept that the society capable of openness, of a certain kind of freedom, is the creature of philosophy or of unconditioned thought. What would be the status of that unconfined thought in the life lived within the horizon that constitutes the (open) society – the society of freest egress and ingress of all things? We may envision two possibilities: first, the migration of elements in both directions across the horizon is absolutely random, arbitrary or senseless, unaffected or unnoticed by a philosophy that looks elsewhere. Second, the power that drew the horizon continues ceaselessly to exercise the same power, continually revising its original draftsmanship, regulating the ingress and egress of elements, standing effectually as the freest or indeed the only perfectly free agent – free by virtue of reason – in the open society consecrated presumably to freedom and reason throughout. The alternative as presented means that the open society is either chaotic and forever in danger of decaying into its opposite without premeditation, or it is subject to the uninterrupted super-intendence of its architect, who never surrenders his prerogative as re-creator. There is no apparent reason to presume that the re-creation will strengthen rather than replace the open society, unless it be argued that the open society is and must be known to be the best political order. But the best political order, *qua* best, is im-mutable, closed, and of eternal or at least natural definition rather than being bounded by a horizon drawn by autonomous human agency. The autonomy of the human horizon-drawer would in the latter case be wholly accidental to the generation of the open socie-ty, which would then rest on chance rather than freedom.

The relation of philosophy and the open society is a precarious one, not because philosophy is traditionalist and confining, but for the opposite reason that it is prone to inquiry and thus to dissatisfaction except in the barely imaginable case that it finds itself in the absolute polity. In brief, the activity we may posit as generative of the open society and thus as clearing it somehow of the imputation of passivity so derogatory to it is an activity of speculative thought, of philosophy whose friendliness to the open society is as fickle as it is to political societies generally. Were the *continuing* activity of philosophy to be the token of the open socie-ty's own activity, that society would stand exposed as a mere for-mality or shell, an occasion for the activity of a thought whose own true love is a restless philandering rather than a fidelity to the system that shelters it in its butterfly peregrinations.

The imputation that the open society, in the mode of the open house, is decisively passive seems hard to shake off; but we have yet to think about another mode of openness, that which is figured in the image of the open eye, that might be more favorable in this or some other respect. Our question now is, What should we think about a society that is open in the way in which an eye is open? An eye is open when a certain barrier is removed between an outside and an inside. That barrier is not like the door of a house, for the door obstructs movements in both directions while an eyelid can restrain only the inbound movement. Moreover, the inside in the case of the eye is not only or primarily the eye itself, but rather the brain and then the mind. Thus, if we were to be able to understand the openness of society by a parallel with the openness of an eye, we would have to be able to find equivalents to the unidirectional movement and the peculiar capacity of the open eye to be struck from without but also to inspect, that is, to take the initiative. Let us abstract from the inertness of the open eye under impacts from without as having been sufficiently considered under the heading of passivity. That leaves for reflection an openness that only admits, and that admits not only the unsought but the actively sought as well. On these terms, the open society would be the chronic ingester of a thing or things we have not named, for the benefit of something residing within which we have not identified. We must try first to understand what class or classes of thing enter or are drawn into the open society, or, to simplify the issue, to what is the open society open? Let us say provisionally that it is open to the ways of others and to the thoughts of others, and it is open also directly to all those things that it might encounter indirectly through the thoughts of others – call this somewhat grandly the whole.

What can be meant by being open to the ways of others? It means to be interested in and curious about the manners, politics, culture, history, and so on of other people, "other" being understood in any way at all. This is genuine but lukewarm openness. Being fully open to Buddhism, for example, would include a disposition to think earnestly about adopting it – taking it in the practical way. In this demanding sense, a serious scholar of comparative religion might have to be described as open to the objects of his study only in the limited or lukewarm sense. In which of these senses can or must the open society be open to the ways of others? I will assert arbitrarily that if it is the essentially open society, then it must be open in the strict or demanding sense. I will not comment on the evident impracticality of openness in this perennially destabilizing sense, were it to prevail in the absence of some influence that would preserve the sheer identity or continuity of the open society. What would the nature of such an influence be? It would be a critical power, capable of distinguishing those alien things that are fit to be chosen and those to be passed over or blamed. It would resemble Plato's ability to contemplate Dorian institutions and find them choiceworthy, perhaps even for Athens. This brings us sharply up against the fact that the power to judge the alien things in a spirit of strictest openness could not function if it were not reflexive, turned inward as earnestly and probingly as it is turned outward. Intelligent strict openness must include introspection: openness to others is defective if its obverse is not a competent openness to itself on the part of the society. Thus we learn that we must make an addition to the list of things to which the open society is open: itself.

What can be meant by a society's openness to itself? I shall take it to mean capable, both morally and intellectually, of the skepsis of its own full experience. But skepsis is a looking, a mere looking as one might say, which is to be perfected in an act of judgment, a pronouncement of good or bad. Judgment entails the availability of standards of judgment. Whence do they come? From the vantage point of the open society – open in the mode of the open eye – they can come from anywhere within or without the society: from strange philosophy, from true or false prophecy, from intuition, and so on. Is there no valid judgment on the validity of the standards for judging experience? The question is not any more pertinent to the status of an open society than to the condition of society altogether. The answer is, I take it, philosophy – again speaking with a limited purpose and thus profanely. Philosophy, or thought, provides the criteria of the criteria.

We have stumbled on a considerable difficulty. Stated briefly, the open society must know itself; it must scan its experiences with a view to their replacement if need be by alien things to which the society is open. We have made the suggestion, so easily as to be condemned as complacent, that philosophy sit in judgment and preside at the port of entry. But if any one thing has ever been made clear to us by our experience, it is that we habitually construe our experience, give it a meaning, under the influence of a system of thought or at least prejudice, and maybe even of philosophy. In the worst case, then, our very experiences would have a meaning that is imparted to them by some system of thought; and we would then go on to interpret and evaluate those same experiences by the application of criteria of judgment supported by some system of thought. Unless we are tacitly referring to two mutually independent systems of thought, we are talking nonsense. And if we are referring to two systems of thought, we are talking about the creatures who subscribe to them, beings who regularly apply criteria to their criteria. In saying these things, I mean to imply nothing about the soundness or the practicality of open society, but rather to say something about the conditions of meaning and existence of such a society not necessarily understood by those who argue for it. I do not believe that the difficulty I have just sketched is in principle insuperable. It seems to me not only possible, but desirable, that there be two concurrent systems of thought simultaneously active in the society: one, the prevailing political animus that embodies and prescribes the social ideal to and for the citizens, and which stands in the highest place as the criterion of experience and the rule of political orthodoxy sometimes called ideology; the other is philosophy proper, the criterion of all criteria. There is no difficulty in conceiving the co-existence of such so-called systems of thought as long as one understands clearly that their co-existence is in one and the same society but not, *qua* supreme, in one and the same mind.

Thus it appears again that the open society is not clearly conceivable without the supposition of the activity of philosophy within it, this time in order to preserve it by imposing checks on what may enter it from without and to assist it in its openness to itself. Philosophy preserves the identity of the open society by providing it with the indispensable closure. The open society belongs to a class of things whose preservation depends on the mitigation of its own essential principle.

Having in this way introduced philosophy as a condition of the open society, I will take advantage of its presence as a means of explaining that society's openness to the whole and to the thoughts of others about all things. Considering the isolation of philosophy from the plane of political orthodoxy as a basis of openness in society, I would say that the open society is sanity incarnate. It is also indistinguishable, in this respect, from good society irrespective of openness. So far as open society does not perceive this about itself, it lacks what I believe is a necessary condition for its own existence, namely, a clear conception of the place of philosophy in political life altogether.

To conclude: in this very brief sketch, I have tried to show that society may be thought of as being open in the way of a flower, a door, and an eye. Its openness in the manner of the flower must be understood as dependent upon a recognition of essence, which means philosophy. Its openness in the manner of the door is tainted with passivity until cleansed by the presence of philosophy as the principle of activity within it. Its openness in the manner of an eye is dependent on the judging and hence closing power of philosophy, without which the open society would for yet another set of reasons lose itself.

It would appear that the preservation, to say nothing of the formation, of open society would depend upon the infusion of a constitution or of a social order with philosophy. Does this mean that men will not live openly until their governors become philosophers or philosophers become their governors? If so, it challenges Plato, whose Socrates gives reason to believe that such a success of philosophy would accompany or serve the closing of society. The authority of Plato is not as such decisive; neither can it be dismissed. The status of the open society might best, therefore, be regarded as uncertain as long as there is any reason to consider philosophy as both indispensable and antithetical to its existence. If the infusion of society with philosophy means the active presence therein of the deepest thought about humanity, one can conclude that the indispensable will not prove to be also the antithetical only by presupposing that open is best, which may not be merely presupposed. That the status of the open society is equivocal might mean that it has something in common with the worst and the best, both of which are destined to precarious existence. We are thus brought to the threshold of the judgment that philosophy alone is competent to render, a judgment to which we cannot here proceed.

How Open Can "Open" Be?

Iredell Jenkins

I shall not at the outset attempt any precise definitions of "open" and "closed" societies: these terms convey little meaning, being honorific and pejorative epithets rather than descriptions. When we speak of an "open" society, we mean one that is focused on its members: we think of the liberties and protections that it affords its citizens, the permissiveness it allows them, its dedication to the ideals of equality and opportunity. In short, the emphasis is on the *rights of persons*. The "closed" society is focused on itself – the state or nation – as distinct both from its own members and from other groups: strength and survival – security and the status quo – are its gods. Control is imposed from a central source, and all members share the same training, undergo the same indoctrination, are cast in the same mold. Status and class are significant features of life. In sum, the emphasis is on the *roles* that persons are to fill and the *duties* they must discharge.

In praising the open society, it is always the qualifier that is stressed: it is the "openness" that we value. We take the substantive, "society," for granted, blithely assuming its presence to protect us and provide for our needs. This is a dangerous simplification, for this necessary basis of our lives, society, must have the attributes of closedness in order to exist as such. All societies were closed for long periods of time before any began to open (China started only yesterday and already shows signs of regretting it);

many even advanced ones have remained closed; and many have opened only to close again. Finally, however undesirable we may think it, a closed society has one great virtue: it can survive. The past proves that. But if a society becomes too open, it either perishes or it re-closes itself in an effort to save itself (Poland is merely the latest in a long line of examples).

There is a second simplification that is equally serious. We pose the problem of openness exclusively in terms of political systems and social structures. We think of it as a conflict between "democracy" and "totalitarianism," human rights and governmental repression. This is certainly an important facet of the problem: but it has at least two other equally critical facets that arise in other contexts. This I believe can best be illustrated by turning to Plato and his doctrine of the One and the Many. This is a theme that runs through every phase of Plato's thought, taking on different guises in different contexts: unity and plurality, sameness and difference, permanence and change, whole and parts, end and means, process and pattern, freedom and order. As a social and political problem, the One and the Many occupied Plato throughout his life, and he returned to it in several of his most important dialogues, notably the *Republic*, the *Statesman*, and the *Laws*.

The problem is simple and stark. The One and the Many are so remote from one another and so incompatible that it seems impossible that they should be as universally compresent and as intimately conjoined as they obviously are. How is this to be explained theoretically? And how are the two to be reconciled practically? I shall first pose the problem in highly abstract terms: these can then be transposed into the three contexts in which we encounter the problem in our search for a balance of openness and closedness.

The drive of the One is inward, toward the maintenance of itself as an enduring and immutable entity—as pure Being. The One manifests itself in the guises of coherence, stability, sameness; its essence is order, and in relation to its Many, it asserts itself and demands conformity. The drive of the Many is outward, toward the ever greater expansion of their existences—as sheer Becomings. The Many manifest themselves in the guises of spontaneity, change, diversity; their essence is freedom, and in relation to their Ones they assert their individuality and demand privacy.

So far, of course, there is no problem: we have simply

distinguished two distinct realms. The problem is created by the fact that each of these modes of reality is dependent upon the other if it is to realize itself. The One can only become actual through the Many, which differentiate and make explicit what was at first closely fused and only implicit. Conversely, the Many can only have meaningful existences through their Ones, which support and guide their passages through time.

This being the problem, the general terms of its solution are again simple: ways must be found to mediate between these alien elements and strike an acceptable balance between their incongruous natures and competing demands. A series of semi-autonomous but related entities or forces must be interposed between the polar extremes of the One and the Many. These intermediaries can cushion the potential conflict of these two, promote cooperation between them, and forestall domination by either party. Put negatively, the problem is to prevent the tyranny threatened by the One and the anarchy threatened by the Many. The difficulty is to explicate these elements and relationships more precisely, and then to effect a solution to the problem in practice.

This analysis has been not only abstract, but remote from the problem of the open society. It will become more concrete, and hopefully more relevant, when I now apply it to the three contexts in which we confront the problem: the political economy of the society, its culture and mores, and its intellectual climate.

Discussions of the open society are focused on the first of these contexts, so here its terms are familiar to us. Politically, the problem is the age-old one of both instituting and controlling power. As Madison put it in the *Federalist*, "you must first enable the government to control the governed; and in the next place oblige it to control itself."[1] The solution adopted by the Founding Fathers was the elaborate segmentation of government provided in the Constitution: the separation of powers in the federal government, the division of powers between it and the states, the limitations on the powers of the legislative and executive branches, an independent judiciary, and finally, the addition of the Bill of Rights, with the blanket reservations of rights and powers found in the Ninth and Tenth Amendments. All of these, along with political parties, are obvious agents of mediation between the government and the people, the One and the Many.

This apparatus has worked reasonably, even exceptionally, well for some two hundred years. But it is uncertain to what extent this has been due to the apparatus itself, to the fortunate and unusual set of circumstances that has prevailed through much of the life of this country, to the fortuitous appearance of outstanding leaders at moments of crisis, or to blind luck. And the system is now showing serious signs of breakdown, due partly to more restrictive external conditions and partly to internal stresses from competing regional, economic, class, and ideological interests. So one would need to be extremely optimistic to regard this aspect of the problem of the One and the Many as solved and shelved for good.

In the economic sphere, our record is a good deal spottier. The problem here is to see that the needs of the society are well served and that the people are properly supported in their roles and rewarded for their efforts. We have largely ignored this aspect of the problem, justifying our systematic neglect by invoking various *dei ex machina*: the market place, the law of supply and demand, free enterprise, enlightened self-interest, and, hovering over all of these, giving them its blessing, Adam Smith's "invisible hand." These forces have never resulted in any reasonable facsimile of social justice, and now they are failing to be even economically and productively effective.

We have, of course, always had an array of mediating agencies interposed between the One and the Many, the national economy and the working population. Based on the obvious principle of the division of labor and hence of interest, these are the groups composed of those who have a specific role and function in society: industry, finance, agriculture, or business; the professions, crafts, and trades; educators, journalists, artists, and scientists. The list is endless. Those persons with shared interests and responsibilities soon organize, in order to speak with one voice and to better serve both society and themselves. Seeking a neutral term, I shall refer to these collectivities as *collegial groups*. Such groups vary over a broad spectrum: they may be large or small, tightly or loosely organized; they may serve one purpose or several; their members may be closely similar or widely divergent as individuals. Familiar examples of collegial groups are professional associations, labor unions, trade and industrial organizations; a college faculty and the executives of a corporation; cultural, artistic, and scientific federations; legislatures, philanthropic foundations and police forces.

It is of the essence of collegial groups that they are Janus-faced:

they look in two directions, outward toward their society, inward toward their members. In the former aspect, they are public and functional bodies: each has a specific role, a service to provide, standards to uphold. Society looks to them to serve its needs and oversee their members. In the latter aspect, they are private and protective bodies: they counsel and serve their members, further their personal interests, and protect them against undue interference and harassment. Their members look to them for support and shelter of many kinds.

These two sets of purposes, values, and standards are always present and well known, even if they have never been explicitly formulated and promulgated: they constitute both the *raison d'être* and the bonding force of the group. In short, every group has a *code*. The character and importance of such codes are made familiar to us in such forms as "the honor of the regiment," "the word of a gentleman," "*noblesse oblige*," the Hippocratic oath, "the frontier code," initiation rites, the "Protestant work ethic," the charters and by-laws of associations, and the Codes of Chivalry and of War – though the last two have now been annulled. And the Constitution of the United States is best seen not merely as a written document, but as just such a code, to be adhered to and upheld by all those holding public office.

Collegial groups are the indispensable agents for coordinating the multiple segments of the economic order and for holding their members up to the mark in their public and functional role. The reason for this primacy is simple. The only other available forces are personal morality and public law. The former of these is too variable among individuals, too easily swayed by passion or self-interest, and too short in its reach. Law is too weak and uncertain in its grasp, too easy to evade, and too erratic in its application to be effective. And even at its best, legal liability does not motivate men positively to act in approved ways, but only negatively to avoid getting caught acting in forbidden ways.

The importance of collegial groups lies in the fact that they are intermediate between personal morality and public law, combining the characteristics of both. It is to these groups that most people feel the closest ties and from which they receive the greatest influence. It is the native region, the social or ethnic class, the peer group, and especially the vocational world – whether professional, commercial, industrial, political, military, educational, artistic, or agricultural – in which people move and work and have their being that puts its stamp most firmly upon them and holds them most closely in its grasp. To the extent that a person honors a code of behavior and a set of values, these are largely the bequest – quite literally the *imprinting* – of those collegial groups to which he is the most attached, upon which he most depends, and which can, if they will, most easily detect his shortcomings and bring him to book.

Collegial groups are uniquely fitted to assure a balance between openness and closedness. When they are true to their dual roles, they can secure social order while preserving individual freedom. In the context of the political economy, they are by far the most effective mediating agents between the One and the Many – the most powerful safeguards against the twin evils of tyranny and anarchy.

In the context of the group culture and mores, the critical issue is that of how close and universal a similarity a society must assure among its members, and how wide and general a diversity it can allow. A society should not, indeed cannot, be monolithic. Human self-assertiveness – the stubborn insistence of people on being themselves and leading their own lives – frustrates any effort in this direction. Furthermore, the effort itself is self-defeating. A society needs the diversity and unpredictability of its members: if it is to adapt, even to survive, it depends upon the creativity, the initiative and ingenuity, the fascination with the unknown and the unexplained, the sheer adventuresomeness and playfulness, that reside only in its members. It is the novel, the startling, the unsuspected, even that which was originally suspect, which often enriches a society immeasurably. And this is always the contribution of an individual who is hearing unheard melodies and seeing unseen vistas. Culturally as much as biologically, a society must be able to draw upon a diverse gene pool: the life of the society is fed by the hitherto hidden idea – the recessive gene – which finds the right conditions and makes itself manifest. A society that becomes too monolithic is soon stifled by its own mass and inertia.

On the other hand, a society cannot allow the diversities within it to become too multitudinous, too extreme in the forms they take, and too stiff-necked to acknowledge any gods save their own. For a society to be viable, it must have a fairly high degree of coherence and stability, and these depend on a framework of shared values, attitudes, beliefs, and conventions. That is, there must be a cultural tradition and a body of mores that are generally respected. Among the more obviously essential components of this framework are a common language, literacy, basic skills and abilities, a familiarity with certain fields of knowledge, respect for the law and for fundamental moral principles and virtues. This framework should certainly be general and flexible, allowing for diversity and change. But the society must be prepared to impose its will upon those who demand the acceptance and support of the social order while refusing to conform to even its most essential moral and cultural norms. Tolerance is a great virtue, and the pursuit of equality is a noble goal: but these are not absolutes. Carried to extremes, tolerance would require that the society accept every group on its own terms, enforcing no common standards but allowing each to live by its own particular culture and mores. And equality would require the society to treat all of these groups as though they had equal merits and claims, accommodating its standards of ability and performance to the particular character and competence of each group. Under such a regime as this, the society would dissolve into a congeries of fiercely competing groups with nothing in common save their mutual antagonisms and their common struggle for a favored place in the social order.

It was inevitable that society should become fragmented into classes that are different in character and function. And it is natural that people should seek the company of those who have the same purposes and standards, do the same work, and follow the same routines as themselves. Persons of the same feather flock together as naturally as do birds: the flock is their home and their tutor. And to adopt another adage, if a society is properly open, people, like water, seek their own level. So each of the agencies that I have cited acts quite legitimately in placing its special stamp – its particular code and customs, purposes and values, vocational standards and personal habits – upon its members. It is their responsibility to prepare these members for the roles and activities, the serious pursuits and idle enjoyments, that are to give content and meaning to their lives.

But these agencies have an equal responsibility toward the society as a One, and they should prepare their members for participation in this larger whole. To this end, they must assure that these members accept the general values and principles of the society, meet its basic standards of achievement, and acquire adequate operational skills and vocational training. To the extent that any institution, class, or group fosters in its members a sense of radical difference, an attitude of alienation from and scorn for the generally accepted code and customs, and a demand for special consideration and concessions to accommodate its particular background and habits, it does a disservice both to them and to the society.

If a society becomes too closed, it stifles the initiative and creativity of its members: then it has nothing to feed on but the past, and it dies of inanition. If a society becomes too open, its members, renouncing any common allegiance and responsibilities, tear it apart competing for the spoils: the Many become parasitic upon the One, devouring it without realizing that in doing so they are devouring their own host.

The intellectual climate of a society likewise needs to maintain a balance between openness and closedness. The life of the mind is a cooperative enterprise. Even the most original and creative person, working in isolation from his contemporaries, stands on the shoulders of the past. Those long dead have endowed him with the legacy of their work: they are his silent partners, whose intellectual capital is the resource he draws on. The solitary genius, like the cave man, is a picturesque fiction.

The search for knowledge and meaning can only be carried on in a structured milieu. Thinking requires a system of ideas and a methodology, expression requires a language and media, and practice requires organization. Scientific inquiry depends on a theory to tell it what to look for, where to find it, and how to explain what is found. Artistic expression needs an idiom, styles, and techniques in order to frame the meanings it envisions. And such branches of praxis as law, industry, agriculture, and political economy tackle the problems of the present with rules, procedures, and institutions that were developed in the past. And underlying all of this intellectual activity are still more fundamental elements: these are the axioms, postulates, and explanatory principles that constitute the conceptual apparatus of thought, defining the terms in which ideas are cast, questions are asked, and answers are framed. So the intellectual climate – the minds of men – must be closed in the sense of resting on principles, theories, and methodologies that are generally accepted.

But, at the same time, this climate and these minds must be flexible and receptive to the new. Fresh knowledge and interpretations are continually being introduced into the established framework.

Such change is usually gradual and incremental: details are added to the body of knowledge; refinements are made in idioms and styles; procedures are improved slightly. What we call "revolutions" are actually well-prepared climaxes: Marx built on a long tradition of socialist doctrine; Darwin had many precursors – including his grandfather – in his formulation of evolution; Picasso worked in a seething cauldron of artistic experimentation; and piecework was a familiar practice long before Henry Ford introduced the assembly line.

The balance between openness and closedness is sometimes upset. Periods occur in which the intellectual milieu is in a state of extreme unrest and ferment: there is wide dissatisfaction with the established order; innovation and disputation are in the air. No common ground has any general acceptance, partisanship is intense, and factions abound. There are other periods that are extremely rigid and intolerant: anyone who deviates from the official orthodoxy is scoffed at, persecuted, and becomes a pariah.

But a balanced intellectual attitude is the rule so long as established doctrines and practices are acknowledged, with inquiry and innovation being restricted to the extension, refinement, and reinterpretation of these dogmas. Trouble arises when some visionary iconoclast probes more deeply and challenges either the explanatory principles and settled theories that are the society's self-evident truths, or the policies and procedures that are its guides to truth, beauty, success, and salvation. When this occurs, the automatic response is rejection of the intruder bearing alien baggage.

Yet it is precisely these basic assumptions that most need to be kept in the open and subjected to scrutiny. Since they are taken for granted, even those who work constantly under their shadow are largely unaware of them. And since they govern the intellectual enterprise as a whole, any inadequacies in them seriously mislead the mind. So it is essential that challenges to these elements should be listened to and considered, unless they are contradictory in themselves and not merely of what we currently believe.

I can offer no simple prescription for maintaining this balance between an open and a closed mind – this attitude that is at once receptive and critical. But returning again to the source from which I have already borrowed, I would suggest that it might be helpful to revive Plato's use of myth. This was a device that he employed with great effect; and he fell back upon it particularly when he was expounding the first principles that lay at the heart of his doctrine.

It is not myths as such, with their figurative and animistic language, that are important. It is rather the mythological attitude and the acceptance of our accounts and explanations of things as only partial and provisional, not complete and final. The contrast that I have in mind is that between *myths* and *dogmas* as the terms in which we express our primitive and hence indefinable ideas, and between mythologies and ideologies as the forms in which we frame our systematic interpretations and explications of things.

Myths and mythologies are metaphorical and ambiguous: they do not pretend to embody any exact, exhaustive, and verifiable account; they are open to change and to new interpretations as more facts become known or as people see more clearly. Those who expound and accept them realize that they are true only in a loose and general sense: the better terms for them are "relevant" and "enlightening." They do not so much describe or explain their phenomena as they lead the listener to look where they point and for what they indicate: then he will grasp these for himself. In sum, myths and mythologies are incomplete, tentative, and hypothetical. Plato perfectly expressed the mythological attitude in a passage in the *Phaedrus*. Referring to his myth of love as a form of madness, he put it thus: "Perhaps we attained some degree of truth, though we may well have sometimes gone astray – the blend resulting in a discourse which has some claim to plausibility."[2]

In contrast to this, dogmas and ideologies are literal and precise: they pretend to present an exact, detailed, and complete account; they are closed to change and in no need of interpretation. Those who preach and espouse them regard them as accurately describing what is the case and fully explaining how this came to be. In sum, dogmas and ideologies are exhaustive, final, and categorical.

The contemporary temper being what it is, I would not for a moment suggest that we return to myths as such: our commitment to physicalist explanations and our conviction that measurement is the consummate way to truth foreclose our understanding them and appreciating their usefulness. But I do think that it would be well if we could cultivate the mythological attitude. As expounded by Plato, this frame of mind represents a nice balance between closedness and openness: it avoids the debilitating extremes of the dogmatic assertion that we already have certain knowledge and the skeptical view that no knowledge is possible, but only opinion. If we can learn to take our theories as having the status of myths – as having "some degree of truth" and "claim to plausibility" – we can rely on them with confidence as sound guides to inquiry and practice. But we will also recognize that they are not – they cannot be – apodictic or complete, so we will be prepared to modify or even discard them when it becomes evident that they are inadequate as explanatory principles and ineffective as practical policies.

And now, "Watchman, what of the night?" Is all well, or is it not? If he heard, I fear that he would report that all is far from well, and that we are doing very poorly in striking a balance between openness and closedness. Indeed, we seem not even to be aware of this as a challenge that must be met, for we give no sign of dealing with it in a purposeful manner. As one consequence of this unawareness, our failure is of a different type in each of the three contexts discussed above. We are unable even to go astray consistently.

In the context of the political economy, we oscillate wildly between the One and the Many: between appeals to big government for largesse and demands that "it get off our backs." And being thus absorbed with the extreme members of the equation, we ignore those indispensable mediating agents, collegial groups. As we have seen, these groups are Janus-faced: they have a public aspect, not only a private one; they are supposed to serve the society conscientiously in their allotted role and to see that their members discharge their duties competently and honestly. But they are failing lamentably to do either of these things. Collegial groups of all sorts, from the smallest and least significant to the most powerful and influential, are withdrawing almost entirely into their private roles. They devote the greater part of their effort to strengthening their positions in the social order and advancing the interests of their members while protecting them against the consequences of their misdeeds. This is equally true of street gangs that wage open war on society, and of professional associations, labor unions, the commercial and industrial communities, the bureaucracy, and public officials of every rank, all of which are engaged in similar wars that are more damaging if less open. It is a rare evening newscast that does not report some case of gross incompetence or corruption by prominent members of these groups. Yet punish-

ment, censure, or even opprobrium are conspicuous by their
absence. Quite to the contrary, it is the "whistle blower" who gets
demoted or sacked. Where all are fools, there is no king, and when
dereliction is normal, there are no norms. And the sad truth seems
to be that collegial groups are becoming little more than benevolent
and protective orders.

As this degeneration spreads, the political economy – the
organizational structure of the society – threatens to collapse.
When collegial groups renounce their public roles, there are no effective mediating agencies between the One and the Many – the
state and the citizenry: so these confront one another at naked
sword's point. Collegial groups become self-serving aggregations
of the Many, each seeking to use the resources of the society and
the authority of the government to further its own interests, with
little or no regard for the common good. The first response of the
One – the state – is to distribute largesse, in the hope of luring its
straying sheep back into the fold. But when this fails, the state inevitably exerts its power in order to impose control upon these
recalcitrant groups and assure the maintenance of the social
order – the survival of the society: restrictive laws are enacted,
security is tightened, civil rights are revoked, and even the courts
now sanction government actions that before would have been
struck down. In a word, as these fragments of the Many – these
decadent collegial groups – close themselves and refuse cooperation while demanding concessions, the One – the state transformed
into a dictatorship – closes upon itself and imposes its will by force.
If all of this seems a deluded prophecy of doom, we would do well to
remember that it is a common occurrence in most parts of the
world. And there is abundant evidence that this country, along
with most Western democracies, is well advanced in the
preliminary stages of this disintegration. The most pervasive
evidence of this confrontation is the sharply increased animosity
that characterizes the relations between the government (the state)
on the one hand and such groups as industry, finance, agriculture,
organized labor, and ethnic minorities on the other. The respective
interests and concerns of the parties, as perceived by them, are so
divergent that they are unwilling to cooperate, unable to communicate, and even incapable of understanding one another's
points of view. Dissension breeds mistrust, and this in turn spawns
paranoia, that most destructive, to both self and others, of all the

passions of the soul. Cassandra was not popular, but she was right.

As regards the culture and mores, our error is glaringly obvious: our society has become excessively open. A society certainly should not demand universal conformity to a detailed body of cultural and moral norms. Individual and group differences are ineradicable, and they are valuable assets of the society: so any such effort is as futile as it is foolish. But there must be a framework of shared beliefs, conventions, and values around which these differences can cluster and which they can reflect and enrich in their various ways. As suggested earlier, among the significant elements of this framework are: a common language; literacy; respect for the law and for the rights of others; a general familiarity with the political and economic systems within which one must live and make his way; the recognition that one must work to be rewarded and that he must acquire adequate knowledge, training, and qualifications if he is to work effectively and be rewarded accordingly; acceptance of responsibility for one's actions and for their impact on one's self and on others; and the obligation to care for one's children. Unless a society is able to establish some norms and obtain a reasonable consensus on such matters as these, it becomes overburdened with deviant groups which demand much and contribute little, and who cannot live or work together but exist apart in mutual suspicion.

I think that our society now faces this fate as a clear and compelling danger. What we have done, in essence, is to render the ideals of tolerance and equality meaningless by interpreting them in absolute terms. Tolerance derives from a Latin root signifying "to bear," "to endure," "to put up with." The idea has two components. It indicates that what is being tolerated is a deviation from the norm, or even the normal, and that it is at least potentially harmful or dangerous. But it also indicates that the deviation in question is not so immoderate and widespread as to be an immediate threat. We now tolerate the widest varieties of religious denominations and political parties, because we recognize that they have common goals and do not threaten one another or the social order, though the conflict of these different views can be vastly destructive, as the past amply proves. On the other hand, it would never occur to anyone who was even semi-literate to say that he could tolerate someone else's preference for vanilla over chocolate ice cream or for serge rather than gabardine for his suits. We "tolerate" only what we recognize as an "acceptable" deviation from a norm.

Similarly, the concept of equality requires a context and a standard by which to determine equality or degrees of inequality. People can be equal or variously unequal in height, speed of foot, wealth, mathematical ability, mechanical skill, manual dexterity, command of the English language, and in hundreds of other specific ways. But they cannot be simply "equal" without qualification. Any such claim is worse than absurd: it is strictly meaningless. As soon as it was a matter, not of justifying the Revolution, but of drafting the Constitution, the rhetorical assertion of the Declaration of Independence was qualified as "before the law." And to judge and treat people as though they were equal, despite their obvious differences in ways that are relevant to the enterprise in hand, is grossly unfair – inequitable or unequal – to the people themselves, and destructive of the enterprise. Yet this is what our society is now doing in one context after another.

In our insistence on absolute equality despite important differences, we accept the demand of people to be taught in their native language or in any dialect or argot of their choosing; we have debased education into a diploma-granting ritual. Any attempt to impose even the most minimal qualification for voting is impugned as intentional discrimination, and tests to determine training and ability for position have been perverted into devices for satisfying arbitrary quotas.

Furthermore, the reason we are acting in this senseless and destructive manner is easy to discern: we are obsessed with a sense of racial and sexual guilt. One would have to be blind, a fool, or a liar to deny that our society, in common with most others, has been guilty of discrimination against these groups. Too much of this still persists; but we have at least confessed our error and have made sincere and significant improvements in our treatment of them. This, however, is not enough to assuage our guilt. And having found that it will be too difficult and take too long to bring all the members of these groups to a position of equality in fact, we have simply proclaimed them equal by definition. So we open roles and positions to all alike without regard for real and relevant differences. And we justify ourselves with such doctrines as "compensatory justice," "cultural bias," and "past societal discrimination." A guilty conscience may be a powerful force for reform, but it is certainly not a sound guide.

In espousing such extreme openness as we now do, we have simply dissolved the One by absorbing it into the Many. A true society is a company of citizens who respect a cultural and moral tradition upheld by various institutions; they are companions who share a civilization. But now we treat society as though it were merely a multitude of individuals and groups, quite indifferent to one another, who happen to be congregating – swarming – in the same area.

In searching for the means to describe such a mockery of society, I think that the most exact term is *lax*. To be lax is to be loose, slack, careless, vague, undisciplined. I have further discovered, through that treasure house, the *Oxford English Dictionary*, that *lax* derives from the same Latin root as the verb *languish*: to languish is to grow weak, faint, feeble; to suffer impaired vitality and vigor; to be depressed and listless; to acquiesce rather than exert oneself. I would suggest that the shoe fits perfectly, and we are wearing it. To borrow the figure of T.S. Eliot, if a society becomes too closed – rigid – in its culture and mores, it ends with a bang of a revolution. If it becomes too open – lax – it ends with a whimper of resignation.

If the preceding analyses and criticisms seem extreme, as I fear they may, those that I shall now advance will appear paradoxical and even perverse. For I intend to argue that the intellectual climate of our society has become dangerously *closed*. I am aware that this must seem an incongruous charge to bring against the present. But I think that it becomes fully reasonable if we simply make a necessary distinction between the very different types of climate that prevail in the two facets or contexts of our body of doctrines and beliefs that I distinguished earlier.

One of these contexts comprises the basic explanatory principles and methodologies that support the intellectual enterprise and by reference to which we organize our knowledge and determine our policies. Defined subjectively, these are assumptions, convictions, and commitments that we never question and rarely even become aware of. Most simply, they are our "taken for granteds."

The other context is vast and miscellaneous: it is perhaps best referred to as "all the rest." It has three principal parts: first, the detailed bodies of doctrine – the sciences – that are based on these principles; second, the general rules and procedures that we follow in our various public and private pursuits; and third, those large and ill-defined areas in which we hold that knowledge is not possible, but only opinion, so that everyone is free to believe, behave, and speak as he chooses.

With this distinction estabished, I can now support my seemingly perverse charge. I do not, of course, question the fact that in the second of these contexts the intellectual climate is thoroughly open: indeed, I think that in the first part – the sciences – we have established as nice a balance between openness and closedness as one can hope for. In the third – the field of what we call "mere opinion" – we are probably a great deal too open and permissive; but that is closely related to the laxity of our culture and mores, and I shall not labor the point. So it would truly be perverse to claim that this vast body of "all the rest" is too closed.

However, the situation is very different in the other and more significant context: that of our explanatory principles and basic commitments. Here I do argue that our intellectual climate is narrowly and rigidly closed. With regard to these elements, our attitude is dogmatic and repressive. Any challenge to these "taken for granteds" is automatically rejected as based on ignorance or prejudice; and anyone who questions them is belabored with such terms of opprobrium as "racist," "bigot," and "reactionary."

But it is just this aspect of the intellectual enterprise that is the most important and influential, and hence the most in need of being kept open. For this controls all of our inquiries and practices, determining the ends these will seek, the direction they will take, the facts they will recognize, the beliefs and policies that will be accepted as reasonable. And in this context, the intellectual climate is doctrinaire and ideological to an extreme. This attitude characterizes all of those groups that are the most powerful in the intellectual life of the society: the academic establishment, the scientific community, political parties, the legal and medical professions, and even the financial and industrial worlds, which we would expect to be receptive to the facts of life. All of these demand absolute adherence to their tenets, refusing to consider any alternatives to them.

As a result of this closed attitude, the intellectual environment is infested with a motley array of stereotypes, shibboleths, and shots in the dark that pose, and are accepted, as confirmed and all but revealed truths. As examples, I would cite the following: our commitment to science and rationalism as the only sources of knowledge; our belief in the innate goodness and perfectability of

man; our refusal to ascribe guilt to anyone, blaming everything on
"society" as the universal scapegoat; the concepts of the ego, the id,
and the collective unconscious; the charming fable of the giant
chemical molecule that stumbled on the secret of self-replication
and thus started the entire evolutionary process; the "big bang"
theory of the origin of the universe; and, at a more practical level,
the competing dogmas of the Welfare State and the New
Federalism, a controlled economy and supply-side economics, with
the adherents of each unwilling to give an inch or consider compromise. Now, I do not mean to assert that all of these tenets are
false or absurd. Most of them are quite reasonable, though some of
them are patently ridiculous; some of them have a very large
measure of truth; the majority of them have been fruitful guides to
inquiry and practice, though some of them have seriously deluded
and misled us. But no one of them is completely confirmed or
thoroughly adequate as an explanation.

To revert to an earlier discussion, I would suggest that these
tenets and doctrines are properly to be regarded as myths, in the
Platonic sense: as he so aptly put it, they probably contain "some
degree of truth" and have "some claim to plausibility." But that is
all. The more sophisticated masters of the disciplines in question
know this. But the intellectual community as a whole, and especially the public, do not. These and other theories and concepts that
are similarly mythological are accepted as complete and reliable explanations, and no other suggestions will be entertained.

Because of our commitment to these dogmas, we are unwilling to
acknowledge, and even unable to recognize, obvious facts. As a
consequence we persist in bankrupt policies that lead to dead ends.
Examples abound in every context of our national life. Since we
have whole-heartedly espoused Rousseau's quaint notions of the
noble savage and society as the great corrupter, any suggestion
that individuals themselves and their families bear some of the
responsibility for the fact that they are unemployable and live on
the margin of society – that they should have gotten some education and training instead of harassing their teachers and
schoolmates – is dismissed as prejudice. Since society is the universal corrupter and scapegoat, society has an obligation to serve as
surrogate nurse, tutor, and provider. In quite another context,
our worship of technology leads us to squander untold trillions
of dollars building weapons that are so sophisticated that the

military forces cannot recruit and retain people with the skill to either operate or repair them. So they lie idle for five or ten years; then they become obsolete, and we sell them to other countries – which frequently turn them against us. Finally, and most tragically, our conviction that we are the ordained lords of the creation incites us to ruthlessly exploit the world's natural resources, destroy countless living species, and befoul the environment and accumulate atomic arms and waste to the point where the earth, the home of all life, stands in imminent danger of obliteration – whether instantly through holocaust or gradually through pollution.

In conclusion, I would like to look briefly at a recent phenomenon that perfectly illustrates this doctrinaire and ideological – this closed – attitude of mind: this is the vehement reaction of the intellectual community to the Moral Majority, and especially to their doctrine of "scientific creationism." I am not a disciple of the Moral Majority, and I do not accept the account of creation given in the Book of Genesis as a sound cosmology. But neither do I believe that science has the vaguest idea how the universe as a whole happens to be here: as Heidegger put it, "why there is something rather than nothing." The "big bang" theory does not even address this ultimate question, since it presupposes "something" to "go bang." If we take the scientific account as wholly adequate – which scientists themselves acknowledge not to be the case – and think it through to the end, there are only two logically possible conclusions: either the universe has always been here, or it somehow and sometime came from nothing. If you try to form a clear idea of either of the "possibilities," you find that the harder you try, the more inconceivable they become. The big bang is a lovely mythological fable: it is great fun to hear the stupendous explosion and to picture the innumerable little bits of matter rushing madly around, with order gradually emerging from chaos and laws of nature being enacted. The event may even have occurred. But it certainly was not the origin of the universe.

Still, the big bang taking place and the giant chemical molecule chortling with glee as it madly replicates itself can be taught to school children, who will of course accept them as actual historical events. But a creative agent cannot even be mentioned, save later in an ancient history class and as an example of primitive thinking.

The term "scientific creationism" is clearly self-contradictory, and the Moral Majority should give over this hypocritical pretense of sharing the methods and prestige of the natural sciences. Further, I have not the slightest conception of how creationism could be taught as a systematic body of knowledge. We can be about as sure as we can of anything that evolution has in fact occurred. Biologists can give a detailed account of the processes through which living forms have differentiated and developed: there are gaps in the record, and a good many unanswered questions, but the broad picture is clear and persuasive. I do not see what the creationists can offer in place of this, nor how they can dispute it as a well-documented empirical account. But no scientist pretends to know exactly and with any certainty how the process was initiated. It may be that there is only the physical cosmos, infinite and eternal, composed of mass-energy dispersed in space-time and subject to a causal nexus. But it may also be that there is "something" that is beyond and prior to this cosmos. And I would think that the creationist could reasonably advance the possibility that there is such a creative agent that lies outside the evolutionary process and initiated it.

References to this creative agent should be ambiguous and hypothetical – that is, open – with the creator being identified with some neutral term, such as Bergson's *élan vital*. The idea certainly should not be presented in the form espoused by Biblical fundamentalists, and if the creationist wants to teach the Book of Genesis, he should do so in the Sunday School of his denomination. But I do not see why creationism in the minimal form described above should not be presented to students as a possibility, as alternative to the big bang and complementary to evolution. It seems reasonable that students might be made aware of both possibilities, the more so as there is no essential contradiction between them. Further, various theories of such a "something more" have been advanced by numerous highly respected philosophers. And the modern ideologues have not yet, as far as I know, objected to philosophy being taught.

If this argument is reasonable, then the attitude of the intellectual community appears quite unreasonable. I gather that the creationists do not ask to have evolution excluded, but only to have creationism included. But the intellectual establishment takes the more extreme step of legal action to forbid creationism: the students are not even to have this presented as a possibility to be thought about. This has the air of prior censorship. And that exemplifies to the highest degree an attitude that is ideological, doctrinaire, and closed.

Our misunderstandings of the political economy and the culture and mores of our society are causing much waste and disarray. But given our resources, we can probably absorb for some time the damage they do. Further, these failures are potentially self-correcting, for as this damage becomes increasingly evident, it may open our eyes to our errors and lead us to change our ways. So these might be considered as merely venial sins.

The closedness of the intellectual climate is far more critical: it differs in kind, not merely in degree. For it commits us irrevocably to a rigid body of convictions and doctrines, policies and practices. To the extent that some of these are erroneous or inadequate, they are self-defeating, leading us to spend our energies and resources in ways that carry us closer to a debacle the more persistently we follow them. Furthermore, this failure is not self-correcting. To the contrary, the clearer and nearer draws the ruin it threatens, the more stubbornly does the intellectual community close itself against any challenge of its ideology. This constitutes the innermost bastion of doctrinaire minds, and they would defend it to the death. The danger is that this is just what they will in fact do. For this is our mortal sin.

Any author should make at least one bow to some previous thinker who has anticipated and would confirm his views. Since I have not yet made this gesture of respect, I shall do so now. The predicament that we now face and the whole tenor of my argument are driven home pointedly in a brief passage from that acute historian, Henry Adams, who was also much given to reflection. In his *Education*, Adams put the issue in this way:

> From cradle to grave this problem of running order through chaos,
> direction through space, discipline through freedom, unity through
> multiplicity has always been, and must always be, the task of educa-
> tion, as it is the moral of religion, philosophy, science, art, politics,
> and economy.[3]

That is what a society and a culture must do. And we are not doing it.

This, I think, would be the Watchman's answer, his indictment of a society that is so intent upon the benefits and privileges offered by openness that it ignores the demands and rejects the responsibilities imposed by closedness. His bill of complaint may be a bit rhetorical and hortatory; but then, it is the function of watchmen to call us to arms against approaching dangers.

Notes

[1] *Federalist* 51.

[2] Plato, *Phaedrus* 265c.

[3] Henry Adams, *The Education of Henry Adams* (Boston: Houghton Mifflin Co., 1918), 12.

Notes on the Contributors

George W. Carey is Professor of Government at Georgetown University. He is a member of the National Council on the Humanities, and edits *The Political Science Reviewer*. Among his writings are *Liberalism vs. Conservatism*, co-edited with Willmoore Kendall, *Basic Symbols of the American Tradition*, co-authored with Willmoore Kendall, and *A Second Federalist*, with Charles S. Hyneman. His articles and reviews have appeared in *American Political Science Review, The Journal of Politics, Western Political Quarterly* and *Modern Age*. He has recently completed a book on the political thought of the *Federalist Papers*.

Walter Berns is John M. Olin Distinguished Scholar in constitutional and legal studies at the American Enterprise Institute, and is professorial lecturer at Georgetown University. A Guggenheim and Fulbright Fellow, he has authored numerous books and articles.

George Anastaplo is Professor of Law, Loyola University of Chicago; Professor Emeritus of Political Science and of Philosophy, Rosary College; and Lecturer in the Liberal Arts, the University of Chicago. His publications include *The Constitutionality: Notes on the First Amendment, Human Being and Citizen: Essays on Virtue, Freedom and the Common Good, The Artist as Thinker: From Shakespeare to Joyce*, and the forthcoming *The American Moralist: Essays on Law, Ethics and Government*.

Henry Veatch is Emeritus Professor of Philosophy at Georgetown University, and Adjunct Professor of Philosophy at Indiana University. He has received honorary degrees from Georgetown University and the University of St. Thomas, and is a member of several philosophical associations, including the American Philosophical Association and the American Catholic Philosophical Association. His publications include *Intentional Logic, Rational Man*, and *For an Ontology of Morals*.

James V. Schall, S.J. is Associate Professor of Government at Georgetown University, and is currently a consultor for the National Endowment for the Humanities. Among his books are *Christianity and Politics, Liberation Theology, The Politics of Heaven and Hell,* and the forthcoming *The Foundations of Political Philosophy.* He has published numerous essays in scholarly journals.

Stanley L. Jaki, a Benedictine priest, is Distinguished University Professor at Seton Hall University. He has served as Gifford Lecturer at the University of Edinburgh, and as Fremantle Lecturer at Balliol College, Oxford. His book *Brain, Mind and Computers* received the Lecomte du Nouy Prize in 1970. Among his publications are *The Relevance of Physics, Science and Creation: From Eternal Cycles to an Oscillating Universe, The Road of Science and the Ways to God,* and most recently *Lord Gifford and His Lectures: A Centenary Retrospect.*

Dante Germino is Professor of Political Science at the University of Virginia. He has been a Guggenheim Fellow, an NEH Senior Fellow, and recipient of the "Z" Society Teaching Award at the University of Virginia. His books include *Machiavelli to Marx, Beyond Ideology,* and *Political Philosophy and the Open Society.*

R. Bruce Douglass is Associate Professor and Chairman of the Department of Government at Georgetown University. His previous publications include scholarly papers in the *Journal of Politics, Political Theory, Political Science Quarterly, Thought,* and the *Union Seminary Quarterly Review;* chapters in F. Canavan, ed., *The Ethical Dimension of Political Life* and S. McKnight, *Eric Voegelin's Search for Order in History;* and popular articles.

Joseph Cropsey is Professor of Political Science at the University of Chicago. Among his books are *Polity and Economy: An Interpretation of the Principles of Adam Smith, Political Philosophy and the Issues of Politics,* and *History of Political Philosophy,* co-edited with Leo Strauss.

Iredell Jenkins is Professor Emeritus of Philosophy and of Law at the University of Alabama. He was a Rockefeller Grant winner, and a Senior Fellow in Law and Social Sciences at the Chicago Law School. His publications include *Art and the Human Enterprise, Social Order and the Limits of Law,* and over sixty articles in professional journals and law reviews. He is a member of the American Philosophical Association, the Alabama Philosophical Association, and the International Association for Law and Social Science.